TRACING YOUR FIRST WORLD WAR ANCESTORS

FAMILY HISTORY FROM PEN & SWORD

Birth, Marriage and Death Records
David Annal and Audrey Collins

*Tracing Your Channel Islands
Ancestors*
Marie-Louise Backhurst

Tracing Your Yorkshire Ancestors
Rachel Bellerby

Tracing Your House History
Gill Blanchard

Tracing Your Royal Marine Ancestors
Richard Brooks and Matthew Little

Tracing Your Pauper Ancestors
Robert Burlison

Tracing Your Huguenot Ancestors
Kathy Chater

*Tracing Your Labour Movement
Ancestors*
Mark Crail

Tracing Your Army Ancestors
Simon Fowler

*A Guide to Military History on the
Internet*
Simon Fowler

Tracing Your Northern Ancestors
Keith Gregson

*Tracing Your Ancestors Through
Death Records*
Celia Heritage

Your Irish Ancestors
Ian Maxwell

Tracing Your Scottish Ancestors
Ian Maxwell

Tracing Your London Ancestors
Jonathan Oates

Tracing Your Tank Ancestors
Janice Tait and David Fletcher

Tracing Your Air Force Ancestors
Phil Tomaselli

*Tracing Your Secret Service
Ancestors*
Phil Tomaselli

Tracing Your Criminal Ancestors
Stephen Wade

Tracing Your Police Ancestors
Stephen Wade

Tracing Your Jewish Ancestors
Rosemary Wenzerul

Fishing and Fishermen
Martin Wilcox

Tracing Your Canal Ancestors
Sue Wilkes

Tracing Your Lancashire Ancestors
Sue Wilkes

TRACING YOUR FIRST WORLD WAR ANCESTORS

A Guide for Family Historians

Simon Fowler

Pen & Sword
FAMILY HISTORY

First published in Great Britain in 2013 by
PEN & SWORD FAMILY HISTORY
an imprint of
Pen & Sword Books Ltd
47 Church Street
Barnsley
South Yorkshire
S70 2AS

Copyright © Simon Fowler 2013

ISBN 978 1 78159 037 9

A CIP catalogue record for this book is
available from the British Library.

Typeset in Palatino and Optima

Printed and bound in England by
CPI Group (UK) Ltd, Croydon, CR0 4YY

Pen & Sword Books Ltd incorporates the Imprints of Pen & Sword Aviation, Pen
& Sword Family History, Pen & Sword Maritime, Pen & Sword Military, Pen &
Sword Discovery, Wharncliffe Local History, Wharncliffe True Crime,
Wharncliffe Transport, Pen & Sword Select, Pen & Sword Military Classics, Leo
Cooper, The Praetorian Press, Remember When, Seaforth Publishing and
Frontline Publishing

For a complete list of Pen & Sword titles please contact
PEN & SWORD BOOKS LIMITED
47 Church Street, Barnsley, South Yorkshire, S70 2AS, England
E-mail: enquiries@pen-and-sword.co.uk
Website: www.pen-and-sword.co.uk

CONTENTS

PREFACE

I started this book with the best of intentions. It was going to be a straightforward guide to researching men and women who served in whatever capacity during the First World War. I would discuss the records and show readers how to get the best from these resources and the related indexes. But somewhere along the line some of the people who were there found their way into the text. Initially I only included my family as examples, partly because I had used them before, but I soon realised three men and one woman could not represent the experiences of millions. So I added in several dozen or so men and women from each of the services and the various theatres of war. Their choice was more or less random. Some I searched for, like Florence Green née Paterson, who when she died in February 2012 had achieved a certain notoriety as the last known person to have served in the war, while others just emerged during the research, like Company Sergeant Major Belo Akure, Nigerian Regiment.

I have tried to avoid the famous and the infamous, although there are three Victoria Cross winners. And I have tried to thread their stories – or what I could discover of them – into the narrative as examples of what you should be able to do with your own forebears.

Of course, each person had their own experience of the war. Some men spent months at the front, while others never left Britain let alone met a German. Some soldiers were like Sergeant James Byars, Machine Gun Corps, a pre-war regular who served in Gallipoli, Palestine and the Western Front before being demobbed in 1919 not having received, his service record suggests, a single scratch during his time in the forces. While others like Philip Forster of the Norfolk Regiment died of wounds within weeks of the outbreak of war (and to add insult to injury the authorities spelt his name wrong on his gravestone), or Staff Nurse Phyllis Pearce who was based hundreds of miles from the front but still saw the awful results of the fighting.

And this is reflected in the records. For some men there are full records, as for James Byar, while for others there is virtually nothing, just a bare entry on a medal index card, as for my Great-Uncle Stanley and Cecil Pike, of the North Devonshire Yeomanry (and even here the local newspaper managed to mess up his obituary completely), to indicate the role they played in the Great War for Civilisation. But it safe to say that if your ancestor wore uniform and went overseas then there will be a record for him or her. However, you are likely to find more for officers and men who fell for their country and for those who served during the first two or three years of the war.

One of the great changes of the war was the acceptance of women in the services, and the increasingly important role women played in the war effort as a whole, although records about women in the services are patchy, and almost non-existent for any woman who did not wear Army or Air Force khaki or Navy blue.

The interest in the First World War has grown enormously in the past thirty years or so. When I first went to the battlefields of the Western Front in the mid-1980s it was just a select few enthusiasts who could be found in the cemeteries or marching along what was once the front line to the bemusement of local farmers and cafe owners. The only records readily available were a few memoirs and the war diaries, which were largely the preserve of academics and PhD students. But as the last veterans slowly passed on so the interest in the war grew exponentially. There were television programmes (most notably Richard Holmes' series of War Walks and Channel Four's *The Trench*), novels (like Sebastian Fawkes' *Birdsong* and Pat Barker's *Resurrection* trilogy) and non-fiction reassessments (such as Niall Ferguson's *The Pity of War* and Gary Sheffield's *Forgotten Victory: The First World War: Myths and Realities*).

But above all there was the inspiring dignity of the veterans themselves, such as Harry Patch and Henry Allingham.

It was natural that genealogists, local historians and military enthusiasts should want to research the men who were there. Fortunately, by the end of the 1990s the records had largely been released, and with the arrival of commercial data providers, notably Ancestry which put much of this material online, it is now fairly simple to build up an idea of a man's service in a couple of hours. This is something that would once have taken Army clerks weeks of painstaking checking to do.

Researching a grandfather's or great-grandfather's military career is now one of the most popular genealogical research projects. It can be a particularly attractive project to undertake, because of the variety of records and advice available. In addition, it can still be an emotional subject, asking how we would have coped in the circumstances. (Badly in my case, I fear.)

This book shows you how to get started on researching men and women who participated in the First World War from Britain and its Dominions. It is based on my book *Tracing Your First World War Ancestors*, which was published by Countryside Books (and I am grateful to their MD Nicholas Battle for his permission to reuse the material), but it has been thoroughly updated and expanded to include new material and my own experiences of research in these records over the past decade or so.

Some of the examples used here are based on papers that I gave at the Ontario Genealogical Society in Toronto in March 2012, in particular a paper on the events of 31 March 1917.

ACKNOWLEDGEMENTS

Thanks to:

Melody Amsel-Arieli; Nicholas Battle, Countryside Books; Sue Cox, British Red Cross Society Archives and Museum; Adrian and Nicholas Lead; Janice Taylor, Archivist, Honourable Artillery Company; Paul Jones and James F S Thomson of the Ontario Genealogical Society; David McCrone for letting me use James Byars DCM as an example; Paul Wilkinson for a couple of illustrations; and Alison Miles for her editing.

As always, all errors and omissions are mine.

LIST OF ABBREVIATIONS

A2A	Access to Archives
ANZAC	Australian and New Zealand Army Corps
ASC	Army Service Corps
BEF	British Expeditionary Corps
BL	British Library
CEF	Canadian Expeditionary Force
CWGC	Commonwealth War Graves Commission
FAAM	Fleet Air Arm Museum
ICRC	International Committee of the Red Cross
MiD	Mentioned in Despatches
MoD	Ministry of Defence
NAM	National Army Museum
NCO	Non-commissioned Officer
NMM	National Maritime Museum
NRA	National Register of Archives
QAIMNS	Queen Alexandra's Imperial Military Nursing Service
QARNNC	Queen Alexandra's Royal Naval Nursing Corps
RA	Royal Artillery
RAF	Royal Air Force
RAFM	RAF Museum
RAMC	Royal Army Medical Corps
RE	Royal Engineers
RFA	Royal Fleet Auxiliary
RFC	Royal Flying Corps
RN	Royal Navy
RNAS	Royal Naval Air Service
RND	Royal Naval Division
RNM	Royal Naval Museum
RNR	Royal Naval Reserve

RNVR	Royal Naval Volunteer Reserve
SOG	Society of Genealogists
TNA	The National Archives
VAD	Voluntary Aid Detachment (member)
WAAC	Women's Army Auxiliary Corps
WFA	Western Front Association
WRAF	Women's Royal Air Force
WRNS	Women's Royal Naval Service

The Long, Long Trail has a comprehensive list of the most common abbreviations you may come across in the records at www.1914-1918.net/abbrev.htm.

Chapter 1

STARTING OUT

Records Online

The majority of records for the men and women who served in the First World War are online. This means that with a bit of luck you can very easily build up a fairly good picture of your ancestor with very little effort.

There are two major commercial data providers with significant First World War content: Ancestry and The National Archives' (TNA) Online Records Service, although Findmypast has increasing amounts of material. In addition, there are a few small databases that appear on a number of different sites. These include:

- Soldiers Died in the Great War.

- De Ruvigny's Roll of Honour: A Biographical Record of His Majesty's Military and Aerial Forces Who Fell in the Great War 1914–1917.

- Ireland's Memorial Records of the Great War.

- National Roll of the Great War.

- Distinguished Conduct Medal Citations, 1914–1920.

- Naval Casualties.

- Royal Navy Officers' Medal Roll.

- Royal Marine Medal Roll, 1914–1920.

Ancestry (www.ancestry.co.uk)

If you are researching the Army then you will probably need access to Ancestry because it has the core material of medal index cards and other ranks service records (see Chapter 3). In addition, they have campaign medal rolls for the Royal Navy (RN) and a large range of smaller databases which could prove useful. They are described in the appropriate place in the text.

Ancestry is the largest data provider both in terms of content and

ancestry.co.uk

sylvialevi

Upgrade   Help

Home | Family Trees ▾ | Search ▾ | DNA | Community ▾ | Help & Advice ▾ | Living Relative Search | Publish | Shop

All *Military* results for *Henry Crozier*

Searching for...

Name: "Henry" "Crozier"
Collection Priority: Only UK and Irish

[Edit Search]

or Start a new search

Narrow by Category

▸ All Categories
▾ Military

Draft, Enlistment and Service	1
Casualties	2
Soldier, Veteran & Prisoner Rolls & Lists	3
Pension Records	2
Awards & Decorations of Honour	5

Hot Keys

n New search
r Refine search
p Preview current record

Matches 1-11 of 11 Sorted By Relevance   View | Sorted by relevance ▸

☐ UK, Navy Lists, 1908, 1914   NAME: **Henry E Crozier**
Soldier, Veteran & Prisoner Rolls & Lists
★ ★ ★
View Image

☐ British Army WWI Pension Records 1914-   NAME: **Henry Crozier**
1920   BIRTH: abt 1884 - Durham
Pension Records   MILITARY: 1902
★ ★ ⭑
View Image

☐ British Army WWI Pension Records 1914-   NAME: **Henry Crozier**
1920   MILITARY: 1919
Pension Records
★ ★ ⭑
View Image

☐ British Army WWI Service Records, 1914-   NAME: **Henry Crozier**
1920   RESIDENCE: 174 John Clay St, So Shields
Draft, Enlistment and Service
★ ★ ⭑
View Image

☐ British Army WWI Medal Rolls Index Cards,   NAME: **T H Crozier**
1914-1920   **[Thomas Henry Crozier]**

javascript:TGN_SM_SubmitFormReturnVoid('wcontainer54906274_widget54906274_m_search__moduleSearchtemplate', 'searchBtn_wcontainer54906274_widget54906274_m_search_', 'searchTxt_wcontai...

Ancestry's results screen.

subscribers, and it can be very good. It is a subscription site: you pay for a year's unlimited access to the data. If you are not already a subscriber, it is worth trying the free fourteen-day trial. Alternatively, access is free at TNA, the Society of Genealogists (SOG) and many local libraries.

However, Ancestry can be difficult to use, because the indexing is at best erratic and it is not always easy to find particular databases. It is hard to suggest a way round this, but if you are new to the site then it is worth using the various tutorials before you do any real research. Otherwise, it is a matter of trial and error. You may be lucky, but occasionally you may have to trawl through page after page of names before you find your man.

The National Archives Online Records Service
(www.nationalarchives.gov.uk/records/our-online-records.htm)

TNA's Online Records Service (which until fairly recently was known as Documents Online) is different to other providers because you pay for each document you download: at the time of writing the fee is £3.36 per item. However, some records (generally non-genealogical sources) can be downloaded for free.

There is a wide variety of sources for the First World War, particularly for the RN, which include:

- Medal index cards (which largely duplicate what Ancestry has).

- Some war diaries.

- RN service records for ratings, non-commissioned officers (NCOs) and officers.

- Royal Marine (RM) service records.

- Royal Air Force (RAF) officers service records.

- Merchant seamen medal cards.

- Nursing and women's service records.

These records can be accessed through the main Records homepage, which includes the Discovery catalogue to the holdings of TNA or through www.nationalarchives.gov.uk/records/our-online-records.htm. This is not particularly easy to use, but once when you have found the individual whose record you want to download it is simple and secure to do so. It is important to remember that you should use double quote marks, such as "Douglas Haig", around the name you are searching. If you do not do so, you will come up with all the Douglases and all the Haigs.

Other Providers

The other major commercial data provider is Findmypast (www.findmy-past.co.uk), and although its holdings for the First World War are growing rapidly, they are still rather disappointing. It does have indexes to birth, marriage and death records for service personnel. Its holdings, specifically for the First World War, mainly consist of databases sourced from the Military Genealogy website. It has an increasing number of unique sources including several databases relating to military nursing. However, it does have a complete set of the 1911 census, and the surviving pre-1913 soldiers' documents which might be worth checking out if you are researching an old soldier who re-enlisted on the outbreak of war.

Brightsolid, the company that owns Findmypast, also owns Genes Reunited (www.genesreunited.co.uk) and has made almost all of Findmypast's record collections available here as well. In the text you can assume that if a resource on Findmypast is mentioned it is also available on Genes Reunited. Brightsolid also owns ScotlandsPeople (www .scotlandspeople.gov.uk), which is the major online resource for Scottish genealogy. There's very little here of a military nature, let alone specifically about the First World War, to be found here except registers recording the deaths of Scottish soldiers in what is called 'the minor records'. ScotlandsPeople also has the 1911 (and other) Scottish censuses. One tangential source is the Valuation Roll for 1915–16 which gives the valuation of property for taxation purposes, listing heads of the household and their landlords.

A specialist provider is Military Genealogy (www.military-genealogy.com) which has a number of databases relating to the First World War. However, Naval & Military Press, which owns the website, has licensed the data to other users so this information is available on Findmypast and Ancestry. There is little point joining unless you do not have access to other sites, although it has to be said that their rates are competitive.

TheGenealogist (www.thegenealogist.co.uk) has the 1911 census and an index to war deaths compiled by the General Register Office, together with odd Army and Navy Lists and related records. FamilyRelatives (www.familyrelatives) also has the war death indexes, a few Army and Navy Lists and material licensed from the Naval & Military Press.

There is also Forces Records (www.forces-war-records.co.uk) which claims to have records on over 2 million forces personnel going back to about 1350 (7 million men and women served in Britain's armed forces during the First World War alone). It is impossible to find out exactly what they have without subscribing, which I have not done. In addition, several of my students who joined have reported that it is not worth the money.

There are several more specialist websites which will be discussed in the appropriate place in the text.

Archives

Old documents and archives are kept in archives. Depending what records survive for your ancestor and how much research you want to do on them, you may need to visit several during the course of your searches or none at all. There are several thousand archives, large and small, across Britain, but relatively few will have any records that will be of immediate interest. If you want to know more about what archives are and how to use them there are a series of Quick Animated Guides at www.nationalarchives .gov.uk/records.

For researchers of the First World War there are three major types of archives that you may want to use. There can be a slight overlap between their holdings, but where this is the case this is made clear in the text. In order of likely importance they are described below.

TNA in Kew has almost all the surviving service and operational records for the three services plus much else besides. In fact, it is the repository for British Government records going back to Domesday Book. This is the first (and possibly only) place that you need to visit, although you may never

The entrance to TNA at Kew.

need physically to go to Kew because so much is already online (with more in the pipeline). In this book assume that the records under discussion are held by TNA unless indicated otherwise.

Fortunately, there is an excellent website – www.nationalarchives .gov.uk – which will help you find the records you are looking for and prepare for a visit. In particular, look out for the series of short Research Signposts and the longer, more detailed Research Guides at www.nation-alarchives.gov.uk/records, which explain TNA's collections for specific subjects very simply. If you are hoping to visit Kew there are some inform-ative pages at www.nationalarchives.gov.uk/visit/default.htm which will help you plan your visit, including the very useful ability to order documents in advance. There are also links to other resources, such as the Hospital Records Database, which may well turn out to be a useful lead.

At the heart of the website, and much of what the Archives does, is the Catalogue (sometimes referred to as the Discovery Catalogue). The Catalogue describes all 11 million documents available for researchers at Kew. The descriptions are pretty general, but usually enough for you to work out which documents are most likely to be useful to you. However, a selection of records that contain large numbers of names have been indexed and these names also appear in the Catalogue and you can down-load a number of records for individuals (see above).

It can be complicated to use, but if you just want to do a simple search type in what you are looking for in the search box on the home page. And if there are lots of results use the check boxes on the left-hand side of the screen to refine your search.

It is also helps to put the search term in double quotes, otherwise you risk coming up with lots of results that aren't relevant. "Douglas Haig" comes up just with results that contain the phrase Douglas Haig. Not using the double quotes results in being told about all the Douglases and all the Haigs.

Regimental and service museums and archives hold records relating to their service or regiment. What each place has various tremendously. The big service museums are the Imperial War Museum (IWM) (for all serv-ices), the National Army Museum (NAM), the Royal Naval Museum (RNM), the National Maritime Museum (NMM) (particularly good for the Merchant Navy) and the RAF Museum (RAFM). Addresses for these are given in Appendix 4. In addition, most regiments have their own regi-mental museum and archive, although their archives are increasingly likely to be found at the appropriate county record office. The NAM also has papers from many of the former Irish regiments that were disbanded in 1922, the Indian Army (shared with the British Library (BL)), and the Middlesex and East Kent regiment (The Buffs).

Regimental archives may include collections of personal papers and photographs, war diaries (which duplicate those at TNA), regimental magazines and registers and records that TNA for one reason or another did not want. What each archive has varies greatly, but one thing is certain they DO NOT have any service records (these are either at TNA or with the Ministry of Defence (MoD)). The smaller archives in particular are likely to charge for research and take weeks to respond as they are generally run by a small cadre of volunteers. However, in my experience they have all been very helpful. Most will allow you to visit, but you usually have to make an appointment in advance. The museum website may be pretty basic (an exception is The Wardrobe Museum in Salisbury for the Berkshire and Wiltshire regiments, see www.thewardrobe.org.uk).

The Army Museums Ogilby Trust is an excellent institution which coordinates and campaigns on behalf of regimental museums and maintains a very good website which links to museum websites and provides details about individual regimental museums at www.armymuseums.org.uk.

County archives (or record offices) are also likely to have material, particularly relating to the impact of the war on local communities. In particular, they are likely to have sets of local newspapers, local government records, school records, large collections of photographs and maps of the locality, diaries and personal papers deposited by old soldiers or their families, records of local businesses and charities. And a few have the regimental archives deposited by the local county regiment. Where this is the case the information is always made clear either on the archive's website or that of the regimental museum. There may also be records of territorial regiments from whom many of the 'Old Contemptibles' came in 1914 and 1915, local agricultural committees which increasingly controlled local farms and what was grown, rolls of honour and files about war memorials, the provision of help to war refugees, recruitment of special constables and occasionally papers of Conscription Tribunals, which heard appeals from men who did want to serve or wanted to defer their military service.

There are also many more specialist repositories ranging from the BL, which is comparable to TNA in size and importance, to company and hospital archives. These are not likely to hold much direct information about the First World War but where they do they will be mentioned in the text.

Many towns have local studies collections which may include newspapers, photographs and maps, diaries and other material. Their great strength is likely to be a card catalogue to newspaper clippings which should include references to those who received medals or who were killed in action. Virtually all the London boroughs, metropolitan boroughs and large cities also maintain a local studies library.

Basic information can often be gleaned from the archives' websites. There are likely to be downloadable leaflets which describe the types of records held including, if you are lucky, something on the First World War. An increasing number of websites include online catalogues which can be searched for particular types of records or records about a specific place. Unfortunately, these are often difficult to use, so if you are not familiar with manipulating search engines and databases you might prefer to visit a record office for yourself. Details of opening hours and other requirements are given on the websites. It is often a good idea to ring in advance to discuss with an archivist what you are looking for.

WHAT'S WHERE?

To find the addresses, websites and other contact details of all British (and some overseas) archives visit ARCHON – www.national-alarchives.gov.uk/archon – which has links to individual archives' websites. For regimental museums, however, it may be easier to use www.armymuseums.org.uk.

The National Register of Archives (NRA) provides a database to collections found at local and other archives in England and Wales (and occasionally elsewhere) and where they are to be found – www.nationalarchives.gov.uk/nra.

They are mainly general descriptions of what is to be found, such as correspondence or papers. For a more detailed breakdown of what a collection holds, you need to consult the Access to Archives (A2A) database (www.nationalarchives.gov.uk/a2a). A2A is by no means complete and is increasingly being supplemented by local archive online catalogues, but it is still a surprisingly useful resource. Some of the better resourced regimental museums and archives have added details of some of their collections. There are also less complete equivalents for Wales (www.archivesnetworkwales.info) and in Scotland the Scottish Archive Network has something similar at www.scan.org.uk.

THINGS TO REMEMBER

- Just because you can't find your ancestor in an online catalogue does not mean that there are no records about him as relatively few records are indexed to this level of detail.

- Not everything by any means is online, so you may well need to go to record offices to look through original material for yourself.

- Using search engines can be tricky, particularly those used by local record offices, so if there are any instructions it is a good idea to read them before you start. And in general the more information you type in the more it will confuse the search engine, so try to keep it simple.

THE WESTERN FRONT ASSOCIATION

If you become passionate about the First World War as I am you should consider joining the Western Front Association (WFA). The Association exists to further interest in the Great War of 1914–18 and aims to perpetuate the memory, courage and comradeship of all those on all sides who served their countries in France and Flanders and their own countries during the Great War. Members are a mixture of academics, enthusiasts and family historians.

The Association publishes four journals and four comprehensive newsletters a year, holds several conferences and now runs an excellent and informative website. At the time of writing membership is £26 per annum.

Other Useful Genealogical Records and Sources

It is easy to overlook the basic genealogical sources of birth, marriage and death records, census returns and wills in researching soldiers, but they are also worth checking out. Of course, many researchers first become aware of having military ancestors from an entry in the census or on a marriage certificate. Most of these records are now available online or are likely to become so in the foreseeable future.

The Census

Census records are an important source for family history revealing unique information about ancestors. In particular, because it was taken so close to the outbreak of the war, the 1911 census is a key source as the vast majority of men and women described in it would participate in the war. Helpfully, it is also more informative than previous censuses as there are extra columns describing the number of children born to a couple and more about the occupation of individuals in a household. This is in addition to material about a person's age, birthplace, relationship to the head of household and any physical or mental disabilities.

The census is particularly important because it provides background information about the people you are researching, which may be next to impossible to obtain from other sources. An example is 21-year-old Eric Roper who was beginning to make his way as a singer. And although she was no longer at home, Staff Nurse Phyllis Pearse's entry in the Debt of Honour Register gives the names of her parents and home address in West Norwood, so it would easy to look them up in the 1911 census.

The census for England and Wales is available through Findmypast, Ancestry and TheGenealogist. The Scottish 1911 census is at

CENSUS OF ENGLAND AND WALES, 1911.

The 1911 census form for Eric Roper. (TNA/Findmypast)

ScotlandsPeople at www.scotlandspeople.gov.uk and the Irish census is at www.census.nationalarchives.ie. Unlike those in Great Britain, the one for Ireland is free to use, and it covers both parts of the island. The information in all three censuses is virtually identical.

Censuses are fully indexed and it is pretty easy to find an ancestor in them. Occasionally, an individual might not appear, either because they were missed off (suffragette campaigners in particular urged women to boycott the census) or because, like my grandfather, were overseas on census night.

The 1911 census is unique for another reason. For the first time servicemen, and their families, serving overseas in both the Navy and Army were recorded. Previous censuses had sometimes recorded men in the RN. On census night 1911 there were 264,000 officers and other ranks in the Army and 130,000 officers and ratings in the RN.

Soldier's names, age, rank and place of birth were recorded. Fred Wilkinson, who was in The Buffs, was based in Singapore and his entry indicated that he was aged 24, single and a private. Occasionally, a private might give their civilian trade. But as most soldiers, like Wilkinson, had really had no trade except soldiering none is given.

But native bearers, servants or civilian employees are not included, nor were British officers serving in the Indian Army. Of particular interest are the returns for Army wives and children. This is the first census for which such records exist.

By 1911 soldiers' families increasingly travelled across the Empire with their menfolk, recreating a Britain in miniature wherever they went. With cheap native labour to do the cleaning, the cooking and looking after the children even corporals' wives had a much higher standard of living then could have been dreamt off back in England. There's more about the experiences of wives and children at www.archhistory.co.uk.

These census returns give the names of soldiers' wives and children together with the length of marriage, number of children and where each person was born. The soldiers themselves were enumerated separately but, unfortunately, there is no obvious connection between the two sets of returns apart from a shared surname. You have to know, or at least suspect, that the man you are researching was married.

To access the military returns, in the appropriate box on the search screen tick either 'Overseas military' or 'Royal Navy at sea' to search only for soldiers (and their families) or sailors.

Another problem is that it is not always possible to work out where soldiers or the family was from the returns. A clue might sometimes be found in the birthplaces of children.

As well as details of soldiers, the 1911 census contains unique information about naval officers and ratings who were at sea or stationed overseas (those in British ports should be listed in the ordinary census in the usual way). The captain of each vessel was issued with a book to list every member of the ship's complement from senior officers to boys. He also includes marines. As with the returns from the Army, the information recorded is less detailed than would be found in the civilian equivalent. However, you will find the ship in which the man sailed, his rank and his place of birth.

RESEARCH PITFALLS

Occasionally you can't find your person, and there are two main reasons for this:

- You may have made a mistake in your research, such as noting down a date wrongly or transposing a service number (5130 for 1530, for example). It is easy enough to do. So check and recheck everything. It is a very good idea to have a file for each man you are researching where you record everything about him.

- If my experiences in researching this book are anything to go by, Army and RAF clerks and Navy writers made lots of mistakes. In particular, names are sometimes wrongly spelt or the wrong initials are given. Staff nurse Phyllis Pearse, for example, is sometimes written as Pearce. But if you have done any family history at all then you will have probably come across various misspellings of the names you are researching.

But occasionally one can come across something more puzzling. 6901 Private Philip James Forster, 1st Royal Norfolk Regiment, died of wounds in Brighton's Eastern General Hospital on 24 September 1914 and was buried in the town's Main Cemetery with full military honours. Thousands of mourners lined the route of the funeral cortège, in the way they would not have done later in the war. He came from Attleborough, Norfolk and the local newspaper contains a long description of his funeral. Although there is a medal index card and service record, he seemingly does not appear in either the Commonwealth War Graves Commission database or the volumes of Soldiers Died in the Great War. However, he is listed there under Foster, and use his initials PJ rather than his full name, so PJ Foster is really Philip Forster.

Birth, Marriage and Death Certificates

National registration began in England and Wales on 1 July 1837 (Scotland – 1855, Ireland – 1864). The system has remained largely unchanged since then.

At the time of writing, certificates in England and Wales cost £9.25 each. Although the information contained naturally varies depending on the event, they all have occupation columns for new fathers, grooms and the deceased which should reveal whether they were soldiers or veterans. Interestingly, you can order certificates for men who were killed in action or died of wounds during the war. However, there is little point as this doesn't tell you anything you don't know already.

English and Welsh certificates can be ordered online at www.gro.gov.uk/gro/content/certificates/default.asp or by telephone on 0300 123 1837. At one time you had to supply the volume and other details from indexes to the certificates, but this is no longer absolutely necessary. Scottish ones are all online through ScotlandsPeople. Indexes to Irish births, marriages and deaths for the period (both North and South) are available through FamilySearch (www.familysearch.org), but you have to order the certificates from the General Register Office for Ireland (GROI) (www.groireland.ie).

Indexes to certificates can roughly place when and where an event occurred. There are four produced each year and these can be accessed on each of the commercial data providers' websites and at FreeBmd (www.freebmd.org.uk). For instance, the index to marriages between April and June 1917 confirmed the marriage of my grandparents (Paul Fowler and Elizabeth Crozier) in Twickenham during that quarter.

Also of interest are Chaplains' Returns and Army Register Books which record births, baptisms, marriages, deaths and burials of soldiers and their families at home and abroad. Indexes to this are at www.findmypast.com and at TNA.

TNA has a small number of regimental registers of births, baptisms, marriages and burials in series WO 156. For the Navy there are similar registers in ADM 338. Findmypast also has details of births, marriages and deaths at sea, including for both the Merchant and Royal Navies for the period of the war. They will tell you the date of the event and the ship on which it took place.

Wills

It was natural for soldiers to make wills before going into action. Indeed, the Army pay book that was issued to all soldiers included a simple will form to complete. Generally, any possessions were left to the individual's wife or next of kin. My Great-Uncle Stanley Crozier's will made in July 1917 simply reads: 'In the event of my death I wish my worldly possessions to be given to my mum Mrs Crozier, 62 Pope's Grove, Twickenham. I should like her to give my gold case to Wyn and to keep the watch and chain herself. All other keepsakes I wish distributed as she sees fit.' I am not sure who Wyn was.

There may well be papers about wills and the disposal of personal effects in the files of individual officers and soldiers. If an individual made a formal will it would have been proved by the Principal Probate Registry. Details were published in the National Probate Calendars, which list all wills proved, with the name of the deceased, his occupation and home address, date of death, the value of the will and who the executor was. Entries may appear six months or later after the date of death. A quick check suggests that about 10 per cent of entries seem to be for servicemen, particularly for officers but other ranks are occasionally also to be found. Private William Adamson Maben of Lower Bebbington, Cheshire 5th Battalion Shropshire Light Infantry, died in France on 14 August 1917. Letters of administration were granted to his widow Ada on 9 January 1918. He left effects worth £168 16s 3d. Of course, the Calendar will include details for men who left the forces but died of their wounds subsequently. Calendars for this period are online at Ancestry.

At the time of writing, copies of wills themselves cost £6 and can be ordered by post from the Leeds District Probate Registry, York House, 31 York Place, Leeds LS1 2BA. In addition, the Probate Registry should be releasing some 200,000 wills for soldiers who fought in the First World War

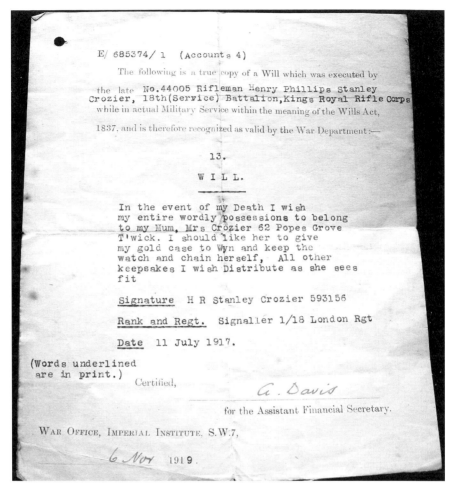

The manuscript will for my Great-Uncle Stanley Crozier. (Adrian Lead)

(as well as in other wars) during 2013. At time the of writing, details of their contents are sketchy.

The National Records of Scotland, in Edinburgh, has a collection of 30,000 wills for Scots soldiers and the vast majority are for the First World War. There is an online index, although you can only see digital images of the originals in the reading rooms. For more details see www.nas .gov.uk/guides/searchSoldiersWills.asp.

In Ireland the National Archives in Dublin has some 9,000 wills. They are online at http://soldierswills.nationalarchives.ie/search/sw/ home/jsp.

Related records are those of soldiers' effects, which concern outstanding

ancestry.co.uk   England & Wales, National Probate Calendar (Index of Wills and Administrations),
1861–1941 Record for William Adamson Maben

Help

Save this record about William Adamson
Maben to your family tree, your shoebox,
or your computer.

Save

↑ Return to Record   1918 > M > Ma > 1

■ View All | ⊖ Zoom In ⊖ Zoom Out | Custom ▾ | 📷 Print | 🛒 Order | ⚙ Options | 🔗 Share ▾ | NEW | ⊕ Magnify | Rotate | Mirror

● What's Changed | Report Problem

Image: [1] of 78 [Go] ↕

MABEN James Armstrong of 42 Conway-road Southgate
Middlesex lieutenant Dorsetshire regiment died 24
August 1918 in France Administration (with Will) **London**
9 November to Robina McLean widow. Effects £160.

MABEN William Adamson of 14 Bromborough-road Lower
Bebington **Cheshire** private in the 5th battalion Shropshire
Light infantry died 22 August 1917 in France Administra-
tion **Chester** 9 January to Ada Maben widow.
Effects £108 10s. 3d.

MABERLEY Eliza Louisa of 7 Berkeley-square Clifton **Bristol**
widow died 9 April 1918 Probate **London** 5 September to
Alexander Cahill Maberly barrister-at-law Frances
Charlotte Maberly spinster and Charlotte Elizabeth Maude
Taylor widow. Effects £5610 1s. 3d.

MABERLY-SMITH the reverend George. See **SMITH** for

MACALISTER Robert Sharp of the Oaks Worcester Park
Surrey died 8 February 1918 at St. Anthony's Hospital
London-road North Cheam Surrey Probate **London** 15
March to Hilda Agnes Walker widow.
Effects £1788 15s. 9d.

MACALPINE-DOWNIE James Robert.   See **DOWNIE** for
MACALPINE.

MACAN Hugh O'Donnaghue of 3 Fassett-road Kingston
Surrey captain East Surrey regiment died 2 September
1918 in France Probate **London** 2 October to Andrew
Charles Lancelot Durham solicitor. Effects £48.

MACANDREW or **KENNEDY** Christina of 21 Bernard-terrace
Edinburgh widow died 16 November 1917 Confirmation
of Duncan Kennedy lieutenant A.O.C.
Sealed **London** 15 May.

The entry in the National Probate Calendar for William Maben. (Ancestry/Principal Probate Registry)

monies paid to the relatives of the men who died while in the Army. They do not list any private possessions returned to the family. These records are with the NAM and can be searched by the museum on your behalf for a fee; they are described in a leaflet *Researching Family History at the NAM* (www.nam.ac.uk/sites/default/files/research-information-5.pdf). However, for officers you are likely to find lists of effects in their personal files. It is less common to find such lists in soldiers' files but I have certainly come across them.

Newspapers

Newspapers remain the least used major genealogical resource, although this is changing as papers begin to be digitised and placed online. If you have an ancestor who was killed in action, won a gallantry medal or even collected funds for a local charity, it is certainly worth seeing whether there is a story it in the local paper.

Newspapers themselves provide a wealth of information relating to:

- Biographical details of individual soldiers, sailors and airmen.

- Individual battalions, regiments, RN and merchant ships.

- Specific battles and campaigns from all theatres of conflict.

- The home front, from recruiting campaigns to conscription tribunals, and the everyday lives of local people, from agricultural shows to magistrate court appearances.

Although the coverage varied between newspapers and depends to an extent on the editor's whim and the space available, you might well find:

- Details of gallantry awards to local men. Often the award of the medal is noted fleshed out with personal details about the individual, such as his family, brothers serving in the forces or their sporting interests. On 1 August 1916, the *Western Times* reported the award of a Military Cross to Captain E W Roper, adjutant of the 17th Royal Fusiliers, précising the citation describing the award and adding that he was the son of Dr C A Roper of Exeter, had previously been an actor and had originally enlisted as a private. Both of his brothers were in the forces, one as a doctor and the other had been wounded on 1 July 1916.

- Weekly casualty lists.

- Memoriam notices. The *Western Times* for 15 September notes that Dr Roper had received official notification of the death of his son Captain E W Roper on 12 September, just three days after Roper's death. No obituary for Captain Roper seems to have appeared in the paper, possibly in accordance with the family's wishes.

- Obituaries of the fallen. These seem to be published between four and six weeks after a man's death. Again, the pattern seems to be to flesh out the announcement of the individual's decease with such personal details as could be gleamed by the paper from family and friends. The obituary for Private Melville James Chapman, RMLI, for example, which appeared in the *Western Times* on 4 January 1918, notes that he has two other brothers in the forces, Herbert at Salonika and Charlie in Italy, information that could only have come from the family.

- Reports on local regiments and individual battalions.

- Accounts of the fighting at the front. Often these are ridiculous upbeat accounts supplied by the authorities in London and bear little resemblance to what we know now really took place.

- Photographs of individual servicemen accompanying stories about them. Almost always these are head and shoulders shots.

However, there are several caveats:

- Stories are likely to be fuller about officers and NCOs than other ranks, partly because officers were more likely to send in stories, and perhaps because editors knew that the upper and middle classes, from whom the officer class came, made up their readership.

- Newspapers are full of errors. So don't take everything you read as gospel. They are at their best when supplementing the archival record. An example of this is the *Western Times*, 4 January 1918, which features an obituary and photograph of a Sergeant Arthur Pike, Devon Yeomanry, who was supposed to have been in killed in Palestine on 3 December. Arthur was a local footballer: 'As a sportsman and companion there was none better liked than he . . .'. I have been unable to find any such person, although a Private Cecil Pike from the same regiment was killed on the same day.

- Newspapers are notoriously bad at following up stories, so a death may be briefly reported one week but no obituary ever appears.

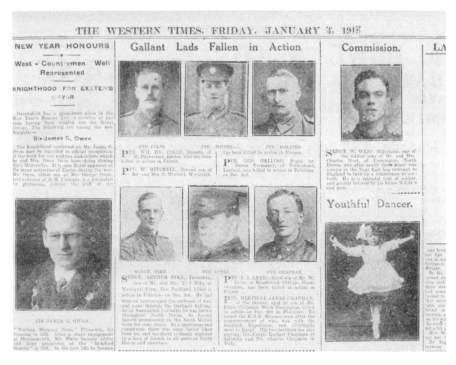

The obituary in the Western Times, *4 January 1918 noting the death of Sergeant Arthur Pike. (Brightsolid/British Newspaper Archive)*

The British Newspaper Library at Colindale in North London holds the national collection of newspapers and magazines. Its catalogue is available online and can be accessed at http://catalogue.bl.uk. The Newspaper Library is moving to Boston Spa near Leeds in 2013 and is at present engaged in a massive project to digitise and make available a selection of papers online. There are several others websites mainly containing nineteenth-century material, although the commercial British Newspaper Archive (www.britishnewspaperarchive.co.uk) includes an ever increasing amount of material from the First World War. A basic search is free, but you have to subscribe to read the whole story.

Back issues from a number of Fleet Street papers are also available online. They are worth checking because they often contain local news. In particular, try *The Times*'s Digital Archive, which is a more primitive version of *The Times*'s Online Archive, although it includes exactly the same material. Many libraries subscribe to the archive and if you have a library ticket, you may be able to access this database from home.

County archives and local studies libraries should also have sets of local newspapers on microfilm.

The 1918 electoral register for Twickenham showing my Crozier great-uncles at 62 Pope's Grove. The subscript 'a's by their names indicate that they were absent voters. (Ancestry/London Metropolitan Archives)

POLLING DISTRICT J. PARISH OF TWICKENHAM. DIVISION II.

(1) No.	(2) Names in full. Surname first.	(3) Residence or Property occupied and also o'd non-resident occupier.	(4) Qualification. Parliamentary.
	HOLMES ROAD.		
2754	aChval, Harry Ralph	7 Holmes Road	R
2755	Rawlings, Percy Edward	25 Do	R
2756	Waller, Benison John	8 Do	R
2757	aFeldern, Fred Stanley	10 Do	NM
2758	aWood, Leslie Frederick Elom	14 Do	NM
2759	Dennis, Francis Wray	34 Do	R
2760	Hensley, Oliver	34 Do	R
2761	Marietto, Percy	34 Do	R
2762	aRobertson, Norman Scott	44 Do	NM
2763	Dover, Leslie	46 Do	R
	KING STREET.		
2764	aWilliams, David Leonard	10 King Street	NM
	POPE'S AVENUE.		
2765	Bordrick, Reginald James	53 Pope's Avenue	R
2766	Adam, Albert Wallace	57 Do	R
2767	aAdam, Charles Harold	57 Do	NM
2768	aAdam, Francis John	57 Do	NM
2769	Wakefield, Stephen Castothow	77 Do	R
	POPE'S GROVE.		
2770	aMiller, Basil Atherstone	5 Pope's Grove	NM
2771	aMiller, Bernard Joseph	5 Do	NM
2772	aDurnford, Frederick Charles	7 Do	NM
2773	aGlover, Cecil Henry	9 Do	NM
2774	aCaton, Arthur Carlisle	31 Do	NM
2775	Fry, Richard Sydney Douglas	35 Do	R
2776	aThompson, Richard James Campbell	41 Do	NM
2777	Stagg, Herbert Cecil	45 Do	R
2778	aFreeman, Stanley	51 Do	R
2779	aFreeman, Cyril	73 Do	NM
2780	Lewis, Hugh Fortman	95 Do	R
2781	Nash, Frank	2 Do	NM
2782	aNash, Horace Edward	2 Do	NM
2783	Day, Horace Percy	6 Do	R
2784	aM'Corry, Arthur Clements	54 Do	NM
2785	aM'Corry, Francis	54 Do	NM
2786	Prideaux, Richard Scott	60 Do	R
2787	aCrozier, Henry Philip Stanley	62 Do	NM
2788	aCrozier, Walter Frederick Basil	62 Do	NM
2789	aCranfield, Herbert Stan ey	68 Do	NM

POLLING DISTRICT J. PARISH OF TWICKENHAM. DIVISION II

(1) No.	(2) Names in full. Surname first.	(3) Residence or Property occupied and also o'd non-resident occupier.	(4) Qualification. Parliamentary.
	RADNOR GARDENS.		
2790	aShepherd, Walter Edwin	13 Radnor Gardens	NM
2791	aGilbert, William Thomas	22 Do	NM
2792	aSimmonds, Albert Edward	24 Do	NM
2793	Hanks, Charles Norman Wait	27 Do	R
2794	aVulgar, Egbert	31 Do	NM
2795	aVulgar, Ernest	31 Do	NM
2796	Fizzey, Alfred	35 Do	R
2797	Reynolds, Herbert	40 Do	R
	RIVERVIEW GARDENS.		
2798	Oswald, Harold Robert	6 Do	R
2799	Thorpe, Harry Oswald	20 Do	R
	RUTLAND ROAD.		
2800	aGiles, William Herbert	1 Rutland Road	NM
2801	Colyer, Frank	13 Do	R
2802	aHart, Frederick George	21 Do	NM
2803	aBlaney, Thomas Henry	22 Do	NM
	SECOND CROSS ROAD.		
2804	Allen, Benjamin John	1 Second Cross Road	R
2805	bBlackford, William Henry	3 Do	NM
2806	aCoster, William Henry	5 Do	NM
2807	aClaxton, John	15 Do	NM
2808	aDodge, Montague William	15 Do	NM
2809	Herbert, Francis	15 Do	R
2810	aSanders, Edwin	15 Do	NM
2811	aMartin, Charlie	21 Do	NM
2812	aBeckett, George	27 Do	NM
2813	aBeckett, John	27 Do	NM
2814	aJones, William	29 Do	NM
2815	aHurst, James Thomas	31 Do	NM
2816	aRussell, Charles	39 Do	NM
2817	aKeen, William	39 Do	NM
2818	aSearles, Arthur Charles	39 Do	NM
2819	Moss, George	41 Do	R
2820	aPotter, Alfred	41 Do	NM
2821	aTruman, William George	45 Do	NM
2822	aGregory, Charles	47 Do	NM
2823	aBradley, Charles	20 Do	NM
2824	aBradley, James	20 Do	NM
2825	aWheeler, John	42 Do	NM
2826	aHurst, William Davey	44 Do	NM
2827	aBeavis, Jack	46 Do	NM
2828	aBeavis, Sydney	46 Do	NM
2829	aGilby, Herbert George	56 Do	NM
2830	aDaniels, James	64 Do	NM
2831	aDaniels, John	64 Do	NM
2832	Glassy, Laban	70 Do	R
2833	aWilkins, James Henry	74 Do	NM
2834	aGray, Bert	78 Do	NM
2835	aEvans, William	90 Do	NM
2836	Potter, Charles Henry	98 Do	R

Minor Sources

Electoral rolls list eligible voters over the age of 21. The franchise requirements were complicated but before 1918 few women had the vote and even
then only in local elections. In 1918 women over the age of 30 gained the
right to vote, as did all men over 21. The rolls for London and Middlesex
are online through Ancestry and Findmypast will be putting up the BL set
of registers for the whole of the Britain in the near future. Otherwise, where
they survive they can be found in local record offices and local studies
libraries. In 1918 service personnel in the forces were entered on separate
absent voters' lists or noted as being absent in the main registers. Often
their service number is given, perhaps with the regiment or unit. A few
absentee voters' lists are online, notably the ones for Leeds. Not all service
personnel registered and not all councils took the registration of local
service personnel with the seriousness it deserved, so there are gaps and
omissions.

Just possibly you may have an ancestor who was either well known (or
became famous) or came from a good family. There are numerous directories and dictionaries that can provide additional information. The best
known are *Who's Who, Who was Who* (which consists of old entries from
Who's Who) and the *Oxford Dictionary of National Biography* (*ODNB*). If you
are a library member, you should be able to access these resources online;
your council website will tell you how. In the entry for Basil Rathbone, for
example, the *ODNB* summarises his Army career: 'During the First World
War Rathbone served as a private in the London Scottish regiment before
being commissioned and reaching the rank of captain in the Liverpool
Scottish; he was awarded the Military Cross in 1918 for gaining information about the enemy.' In addition, there are a large number of specialist
and trade directories, generally for the professions, which will give more
background to a man's career and may well mention his time in the
services.

USING PROFESSIONAL RESEARCHERS

There may come a time when you become stuck or bewildered by your
research. One solution might be to employ a professional researcher
to help sort things out. There are a number of specialists who can help.
But before you contact them you need to be clear in your own mind
what you expect them to do.

Lists of such people can be found on TNA's website (www
.nationalarchives.gov.uk/records/paid_research.htm) and at www
.armymuseums.org.uk. There is also a professional association of
reputable researchers which lists members on its website at
www.agra.org.uk.

> Debbie Beavis has provided helpful advice about employing researchers at www.mariners-l.co.uk/ResChoosingResearcherKew .html.

Further Reading

Books

Simon Fowler, *Tracing Your Ancestors*, Pen & Sword, 2010 offers a succinct introduction to the major sources for researching family history.

The British Newspaper Library has an excellent online guide, *Family History Research and British Military History, 1801–1945*, at www.bl.uk/ reshelp/findhelprestype/news/britmilhist/famhistresearch/familyhist britmil.html.

Chapter 2

CASUALTIES

Introduction

Just over 700,000 British men and a few dozen women were killed during the First World War and many hundreds of thousands more received some form of medical treatment. The vast majority of casualties occurred to officers and other ranks in the British Army. The official figures prepared in 1922 are listed in the table below.

The loss of so many young men was a truly traumatic event, not just for their families but also for British society as a whole. From the outbreak of war there was a determination to commemorate their sacrifice. Unofficial shrines soon appeared in many working class neighbourhoods recording the loss of men from the area, and lists of casualties and obituaries appeared in newspapers. This was officially recognised in May 1917 with the establishment of the Imperial War Graves Commission (now the Commonwealth War Graves Commission (CWGC)) to preserve the memory of those who fell both in paper records and in stone through gravestones and cemeteries.

Within a few years of the Armistice, almost every town, village, church and chapel had its memorial to the men who did not return. There were just thirty-two villages – known as the thankful or blessed villages – where not a life was lost in the service of the Crown.

In 1921, the War Office published eighty-one volumes of Soldiers Died

	Number of Deaths			Number of Wounds			Number of Prisoners of War		
Service	Officers	Other Ranks	TOTAL	Officers	Other Ranks	TOTAL	Officers	Other Ranks	TOTAL
Army	37,452	664,958	702,410	79,445	1,583,180	1,662,625	6,482	163,907	170,289
Dominions, etc.	9,251	196,710	205,961	18,580	409,007	427,587	925	20,338	20,763

(Source: Statistics of the Military Effort of the British Empire during the Great War (HMSO, 1922), p. 237)

in the Great War with personal details of officers and other ranks. And there were many unofficial rolls of honour.

And nearly a century on these memorials and cemeteries still have the power to move and the records, while often very informative, can be curiously difficult when it comes to finding out exactly when, where and how a man was killed or died of his wounds.

If you are researching seamen or airmen, there may be additional resources given in Chapters 6 and 7 respectively.

War Graves

Every British and Commonwealth service man or woman who died during the First World War will be marked in some way by the CWGC. By the Armistice, 587,000 graves had been identified and a further 559,000 casualties were registered as having no known grave. Even today bodies are

The Jerusalem Cemetery maintained by the CWGC in Israel. (Melody Amsel-Arieli)

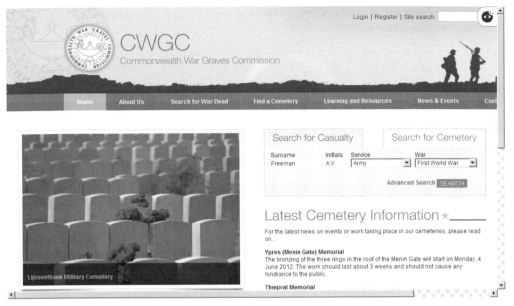

The CWGC website's home page. (CWGC)

still being recovered, such as 250 British and Australian soldiers who were found in a mass grave near Fromelles on the Somme in 2008, and who were reburied at a new cemetery near the village in July 2010.

The Commission is perhaps best known for the hundreds of carefully tended, and very moving, cemeteries scattered through northern France and Belgium, although it maintains cemeteries in 150 countries across the world. You can find out a lot more about its work and its history on its website www.cwgc.org.

The Commission's database of war deaths, occasionally still called the Debt of Honour Register, is also on the website. It is one of the key resources for First World War research and is very easy to use. You can search by name, regiment or cemetery or filter searches by service, nationality or year of death. Unfortunately, it does not include details of the 2,000 or so civilians who were killed in air raids on Britain, as these were then outside the scope of the Commission's work.

For each individual the Register will tell you:

- The name that appears on the gravestone or memorial (generally his full name, but not always).

- The date of his death as it was reported to the Commission.

- His age (if known) and nationality.

- Rank, service number (if appropriate) and the unit to which he belonged.

- The cemetery and the plot number where he is buried or for men like Private William Adamson Maben, who have no known grave, the plaque on the memorials to the missing on which his name has been engraved.

You should always click on the red link on the individual's name as there will in theory be more information about him, as well as about the cemetery or memorial where he is commemorated. There are often notes about his parents or wife, any special inscription chosen by the family for his grave or perhaps whether he was attached to another regiment at the time of death. This additional information may well have been supplied by the family as the Commission contacted the relatives to give them the opportunity to add personal details. For 2/Lieutenant Ivar Campbell, for example, there is a note that he was the 'son of Lord and Lady George Campbell of Strachur Park, Argyll, and 2 Bryanston Square, London' and for Private William Adamson Maben that he was the 'son of Thomas and Margaret Maben, of 63 Stradella Rd, Herne Hill, London; husband of Ada Maben, of 14 Bromborough Rd., Bebington, Cheshire' attached to the King's Shropshire Light Infantry.

Name	Rank	Service Number	Date of Death	Age	Regiment / Service	Service Country	Grave / Memorial Reference	Cemetery / Memorial Name
PIKE, C	Private	242322	03/04/1917		Worcestershire Regiment	United Kingdom	I. A. 14.	PERONNE COMMUNAL CEMETERY EXTENSION
PIKE, C	Private	345695	03/12/1917		Devonshire Regiment	United Kingdom	Y. 71.	JERUSALEM WAR CEMETERY
PIKE, C E H	Rifleman	9509	13/02/1915	19	London Regiment (London Rifle Brigade)	United Kingdom	III. C. 7.	LONDON RIFLE BRIGADE CEMETERY
PIKE, C H	Private	88418	29/12/1919	22	Manchester Regiment	United Kingdom	A. 133.	WITHYCOMBE RALEIGH (ST. JOHN IN THE WILDERNESS) CHURCHYARD
PIKE, C W	Lieutenant		08/10/1916		Canadian Infantry	Canadian	I. D. 1.	SUNKEN ROAD CEMETERY, CONTALMAISON
PIKE, CECIL FRANCIS BROWNE	Lieutenant Colonel		15/03/1920	52	Royal Engineers	United Kingdom	K. A. 35.	FALMOUTH CEMETERY, CORNWALL
PIKE, CHARLES	Private	18393	16/06/1915	28	Wiltshire Regiment	United Kingdom	Panel 53.	YPRES (MENIN GATE) MEMORIAL
PIKE, CHARLES	Private	8256	19/06/1915		Northumberland Fusiliers	United Kingdom	Panel 8 and 12.	YPRES (MENIN GATE) MEMORIAL
PIKE, CHARLES ARTHUR	Private	5076	12/10/1917	19	Australian Infantry, A.I.F.	Australian	Panel 7 - 17 - 23 - 25 - 27 - 29 - 31.	YPRES (MENIN GATE) MEMORIAL
PIKE, CHARLES GEORGE	Serjeant	8615	19/07/1916	59	Royal Fusiliers	United Kingdom	Screen Wall. 3 Gen. B. 257.	GREENWICH CEMETERY
PIKE, CHARLES HENRY	Private	203759	22/09/1918	31	Royal Berkshire Regiment	United Kingdom	V. A. 6.	EPEHY WOOD FARM CEMETERY, EPEHY

Search filter panel: War — First World War; Date of death: (starting); Date of death: (ending); Served with — United Kingdom Forces, Australian Forces, New Zealand Forces, Canadian Forces, Indian Forces, South African Forces; Served in — ☑ Army, Air Force, Navy, Merchant Navy, Civilian War Dead, Miscellaneous; Rank; Service Number.

The results of a search for C Pike, who died during the First World War. (CWGC)

You are here: Home ▸ Search for War Dead ▸ Casualty Details

▸ How to Find a Casualty
▸ Your Results
› Casualty Details
  ▸ Photographic Request
  ▸ Amending Records

◂ Return to results
☐ View certificate

Casualty details

PIKE, C

Rank:	Private
Service No:	345695
Date of Death:	03/12/1917
Regiment/Service:	Devonshire Regiment
	16th (Royal Devon and R. North Devon Yeomanry) Bn.
Grave Reference	Y. 71.
Cemetery	JERUSALEM WAR CEMETERY

Additional Information:

JERUSALEM WAR CEMETERY

Country:	Israel and Palestine (including Gaza)
Locality:	

Find out more about this Cemetery including, visiting information, reports and plans and any emergency notices.

Find out more ▸

The record for Private C Pike, Devonshire Regiment. (CWGC)

Ancestry has what it calls the British Commonwealth War Graves Registers, 1914–1919 which comprise 106 registers from 250 cemeteries. These are in effect early drafts of entries which appear in the Debt of Honour Register. In virtually all cases the information is identical.

INTERPRETING BURIAL LOCATIONS

The number of the plot in any CWGC cemetery is indicated by a Roman numeral following the entry, the row by a capital letter and the grave by a number. Thus, II. B. 28 indicates plot II, row B, grave 28. In the registers of cemeteries that are not divided into plots the row is indicated by a capital letter following the entry and the grave by a number. Thus, D. 12 indicates Row D, Grave 12 (taken from the Preface to British Commonwealth War Graves Registers on Ancestry).

PHOTOGRAPHING WAR GRAVES

It is sometimes possible to obtain photographs of war graves without visiting the cemetery. There are several services that will do this for you. Undoubtedly the best is the War Graves Photographic Project (http://twgpp.org) which is aiming to photograph all British and

---

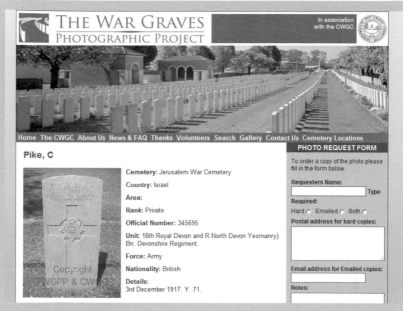

The War Graves Photographic Project website with the entry for Private C Pike in the Jerusalem War Cemetery.

Commonwealth war graves from the two world wars. At present some 1.75 million gravestones around the world have been captured in this way by teams of assiduous volunteers. The website includes an index which allows you to see whether there is already a photo of the grave you are interested in. If there is, you can call you up a low-resolution image of the gravestone. You can also obtain a high-resolution image of the stone for a donation. They recommend a very reasonable £3.50. More details are, of course, on the website.

If at all possible, you should endeavour to visit the grave for yourself (see Appendix 1). Those along the Western Front are easily accessible by car. The CWGC website gives you full details and the exact location of the gravestone, which can be very useful in the larger cemeteries like Tyne Cot near Ypres, where there are nearly 12,000 graves. Photographs of many cemeteries and short biographies of a few of the men buried there can be found at www.ww1cemeteries.com.

Occasionally however your journey might prove to be rather more adventurous. If you want to visit Grave Island, Zanzibar, where twenty-four petty officers and men of HMS *Pegasus* killed during an action with the German battleship *Königsberg* on 20 September 1914 are buried, the Commission suggests:

The grave of Private Cecil Pike in the Jerusalem War Cemetery. (Melody Amsel-Arieli)

Grave Island (also called Chapwani Island) is one of several very small coral islands located a short distance off the coast of Zanzibar and is accessible by privately hired water transport, a journey of 15 to 20 minutes (and usually means getting your feet wet). Take a small boat from Stone Town across to Grave Island. On nearing the island a long low white wall will be visible with steps in the centre. Land near here and climb the steps into the neglected naval cemetery. To the rear and over the boundary wall will be seen the CWGC plot complete with a central memorial to the 24 casualties who have headstones on either side. It should be noted that there are no landing stages and visitors will normally have to wade out to, and in from, the boat. Visitors at low tide will also have to walk 50 metres or more across mud and very slippery rocks. Appropriate dress and beach shoes should be worn.

Fortunately an intrepid volunteer from the War Graves Photographic Project has already made the journey.

Rolls of Honour

Soldiers Died in the Great War

Details of 41,000 officers and 662,000 soldiers who died between 4 August 1914 and 31 December 1919 are recorded in the eighty-one volumes of Soldiers Died in the Great War. This was undertaken after the end of the war by the War Office. To an extent it duplicates the Debt of Honour Register, but Soldiers Died contains additional details, notably the place and date of enlistment and home address, which are not given in the Register, so it is definitely worth looking at.

Information listed about an individual may include:

- Name, rank and number.
- Birthplace.
- Where they enlisted.
- Home town.
- Regiment and battalion.
- Type of casualty, usually 'killed in action'.
- Date of death.
- Theatre of war where the individual died, generally Western Europe. Occasionally a place of death is also given.

The entry for Stanley Crozier reads:

Name:	**Henry Phillip Stanley Crozier**
Birth Place:	Teddington, Surrey
Residence:	Twickenham, Middx.
Death Date:	26 Oct 1918
Death Location:	France & Flanders
Enlistment Location:	Whitehall, Middx.
Rank:	Rifleman
Regiment:	King's Royal Rifle Corps
Battalion:	18th Battalion
Number:	R/44005
Type of Casualty:	Killed in action
Theatre of War:	Western European Theatre

The entry is online at both Ancestry and Findmypast. However, if you are doing serious research on casualties from a particular place or unit or who fell during a particular campaign, you need to look out for the CD, published by the Naval & Military Press, which allows you to search by place, unit or date. Local libraries, family history society research centres and WFA branches should also have sets.

Unfortunately, there is no equivalent for airmen and sailors. However, for the RN there is an unofficial list provided by Naval History Net (http://naval-history.net). It is arranged by individual or by date (so, if you want, you can see everybody who was killed in a particular action). Entries are fairly brief and may not tell you anything you hadn't already found out from the Commonwealth War Graves Commission website. Ernest Highams' entry reads:

HIGHAMS, Ernest E, Petty Officer, 162971 (Dev), Pegasus, 20 September 1914, ship lost.

And for the poet Rupert Brooke

BROOKE, Rupert C, Ty/Sub Lieutenant, RNVR, Hood Battalion, RND, 23 April 1915, illness in Greece.

General Rolls of Honour

One phenomenon of the war was the roll of honour: a published list of the deceased (and occasionally other groups of servicemen such as prisoners of war). Rolls were often produced by workplaces (such as local councils and railway companies), chapels and small communities. They are definitely worth looking out for, although in most cases the information they contain can be obtained just as easily from the CWGC or Soldiers Died in the Great War databases. However, occasionally they may tell you something about where a soldier worked or lived.

The London and North Western Railway, for example, gave families of their employees who died on war service a handsomely produced book, listing the names of those who had made the ultimate sacrifice with details of their jobs, where they worked and their rank (but no unit). Entries for individuals in Coventry's 'Roll of the Fallen' include unit, date and place of birth, place of residence, occupation, date of enlistment, date and place of death and in many cases place of burial. In Scotland the Roll of Honour of Members and Apprentices of the Society of Writers to his Majesty's Signet lists everybody who served with their peacetime addresses and details of wartime service. The information includes theatre of war, wounds received, battles and engagements fought and other pertinent information. Those who died are included in this overall list but they are also shown in a separate roll.

A number of rolls are now online (including the one for the LNWR at www.lnwrs.org.uk/SHG/RollHon/index.php). The website www.roll-of-honour.com has some rolls or links to websites which have put them up, but no means all. It is particularly strong for East Anglia. The Freemasons have been researching the nearly 3,500 Masons who died during the war with some interesting results, which can be viewed at www.masonicgreat-warproject.org.uk.

There is no nationwide set of these rolls, although the IWM and BL Library almost certainly have the largest collections. Archives and local studies libraries may have copies of ones for their area. TNA, for example, has several for railway companies including the Midland Railway (RAIL 491/1259), London, Brighton and South Coast Railway (RAIL 414/761) and the North Eastern Railway (RAIL 527/993). Some rolls for schools are with SOG. And a number have been republished by the Naval & Military Press (www.naval-military-press.com).

There are several larger national rather than local rolls. Entries for some 26,000 officers and other ranks (including 7,000 photographs) were collected and published in 1917 by the Marquis Melville de Ruvigny, a noted genealogist. *De Ruvigny's Roll of Honour: A Biographical Record of His Majesty's Military and Aerial Forces Who Fell in the Great War 1914–1917* has been reprinted by the Naval & Military Press and is available online at Ancestry and Findmypast. You can also download copies of volumes one and two (out of a total of five) from the Internet Archive (www.archive.org). Entries can be very full and in many cases were clearly supplied by the family. That for Ivar Campbell reads:

Campbell, Ivar, 2nd Lieut, 3rd (Reserve) Battn, Princess Louise's (Argyll and Sutherland Highlanders) only s. of the late Lord George Granville Campbell. Lieut., RN by his wife. Sybil Lascelles (2. Bryanston Square, W.). only dau of the late James Brace Alexander; and gdson. of the 8th Duke of Argyll; b. 2 Bryanston Square. London, W. 14 May, 1890; educ. Stone House, Broadstairs; Eton, and Christ Church, Oxford; was an honorary Attaché at the Washington Embassy; on the outbreak of war he tried to enlist, but was rejected owing to defective eyesight; he then joined the American Ambulance with his own car. and acted as chauffeur in France for about three months, until invalided to England with an injured knee-cap; gazetted 2nd Lieut, in 3rd Argyll and Sutherland Highlanders Feb. 1915, and served in France attached to the 1st Seaforth Highlanders; thence went to Mesopotamia, and died 8 Jan. 1916, of wounds received in action at the Battle of Sheikh Saad. River Tigris, on the previous day. Buried on the banks of that river; unm[arried].

If you are researching Irish soldiers it is worth looking at *Ireland's Memorial Records of the Great War*, which is available on Ancestry and Findmypast (and as a CD from Eneclann – www.eneclann.ie). The eight volumes of *Ireland's Memorial Records* were created in the early 1920s to

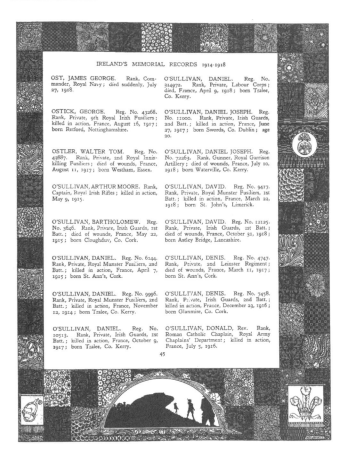

IRELAND'S MEMORIAL RECORDS 1914-1918

OST, JAMES GEORGE. Rank, Commander, Royal Navy; died suddenly, July 27, 1918.

OSTICK, GEORGE. Reg. No. 43268. Rank, Private, 9th Royal Irish Fusiliers; killed in action, France, August 16, 1917; born Retford, Nottinghamshire.

OSTLER, WALTER TOM. Reg. No. 43887. Rank, Private, 2nd Royal Inniskilling Fusiliers; died of wounds, France, August 11, 1917; born Westham, Essex.

O'SULLIVAN, ARTHUR MOORE. Rank, Captain, Royal Irish Rifles; killed in action, May 9, 1915.

O'SULLIVAN, BARTHOLOMEW. Reg. No. 3646. Rank, Private, Irish Guards, 1st Batt.; died of wounds, France, May 22, 1915; born Cloughduv, Co. Cork.

O'SULLIVAN, DANIEL. Reg. No. 6144. Rank, Private, Royal Munster Fusiliers, 2nd Batt.; killed in action, France, April 7, 1915; born St. Ann's, Cork.

O'SULLIVAN, DANIEL. Reg. No. 9996. Rank, Private, Royal Munster Fusiliers, 2nd Batt.; killed in action, France, November 12, 1914; born Tralee, Co. Kerry.

O'SULLIVAN, DANIEL. Reg. No. 10513. Rank, Private, Irish Guards, 1st Batt.; killed in action, France, October 9, 1917; born Tralee, Co. Kerry.

O'SULLIVAN, DANIEL. Reg. No. 314972. Rank, Private, Labour Corps; died, France, April 9, 1918; born Tralee, Co. Kerry.

O'SULLIVAN, DANIEL JOSEPH. Reg. No. 11000. Rank, Private, Irish Guards, 2nd Batt.; killed in action, France, June 27, 1917; born Swords, Co. Dublin; age 20.

O'SULLIVAN, DANIEL JOSEPH. Reg. No. 72263. Rank, Gunner, Royal Garrison Artillery; died of wounds, France, July 10, 1918; born Waterville, Co. Kerry.

O'SULLIVAN, DAVID. Reg. No. 9417. Rank, Private, Royal Munster Fusiliers, 1st Batt.; killed in action, France, March 22, 1918; born St. John's, Limerick.

O'SULLIVAN, DAVID. Reg. No. 12125. Rank, Private, Irish Guards, 1st Batt.; died of wounds, France, October 31, 1918; born Astley Bridge, Lancashire.

O'SULLIVAN, DENIS. Reg. No. 4747. Rank, Private, 2nd Leinster Regiment; died of wounds, France, March 11, 1917; born St. Ann's, Cork.

O'SULLIVAN, DENIS. Reg. No. 7458. Rank, Private, Irish Guards, 2nd Batt.; killed in action, France, December 23, 1916; born Glanmire, Co. Cork.

O'SULLIVAN, DONALD, Rev. Rank, Roman Catholic Chaplain, Royal Army Chaplains' Department; killed in action, France, July 5, 1916.

45

A page from Ireland's Memorial Records of the Great War. (Findmypast)

preserve and commemorate the memory of the thousands of Irishmen who died during the war. The volumes cover the entire island of Ireland, North and South, and contain the names of nearly 50,000 individuals. Also included are men from other parts of the British Isles who served with Irish regiments. The actual details recorded vary from man to man, but you should expect to find rank, regiment and regimental number, and for most men place of birth are given. In many cases place and cause of death are also recorded. It is also beautifully put together with sixteen separate page designs by a renowned artist of the period Harry Clarke.

War Memorials

After the war some tens of thousands of war memorials were erected in honour of men who did not return. They are still common features in towns and villages. As well as those commemorating the dead from a particular town or area, there are many memorials in schools, churches or work

The unveiling of the war memorial at Dodworth near Barnsley on a wet day in May 1923. (Taylor Collection)

places. I came across one a few years ago dedicated to the Milkmen of the Thames Valley in a local hospital. They take a variety of forms – the most common is a memorial cross or a statue of a soldier, but they vary from playing fields to hospital beds and brass plaques. The Holiday Inn, which now occupies the Great Central Railway's hotel in Sheffield, has a memorial book in the foyer to men from the railway who fell during the war.

An ancestor may appear on several town or parish memorials, or in rare cases may have been missed off altogether either because the organisers forgot or the family did not want the man to be so commemorated. Stanley Crozier, for example, appears on both the Twickenham and Teddington memorials. Normally, all you will find is his name, but sometimes also the rank and unit and details of gallantry medals. In small villages everybody who served in the forces may be listed, not just the deceased. On plaques, however, all you are likely to get is a general text commemorating the fallen.

The UK National Inventory of War Memorials, at the IWM, has prepared a database of memorials at www.ukniwm.org.uk. It includes some 55,000 memorials for all wars from medieval times up to the Korean War and more recent conflicts. You can search by place or by type of memorial or even by war. The results can include a full transcript of the dedication and a physical description of the memorial and an account of why and how it came to be created. Sometimes there is a photograph as well.

Unfortunately, however, there is no national list showing which men and women appear on which memorial – indeed, such a project would be an ideal one to mark the centenary. That said, the Inventory does include many plaques and other memorials for individuals, although they are mainly for officers. Even so, it is probably worth checking on the off-chance. There is also an interesting blog on the theme of war memorials in general at http://ukniwm.wordpress.com.

If you are researching an Irish soldier then the Irish War Memorials website (www.irishwarmemorials.ie) may be able to help. It lists many memorials to the fallen both North and South and there are indexes both to individuals and places.

There's long been an interest in the men who appear on the memorials. Studies have been done of a surprising number of war memorials ranging from villages to large cities. Increasingly, the results are available online and it is worth asking in your local library to see whether one has been done for your area.

Here are a few examples. Christ Church College in Oxford has researched men from the college who fell in the First World War. They include a full biography of 2nd Lieutenant Ivar Campbell with examples of his rather dubious poetry (www.chch.ox.ac.uk/cathedral/memorials/WW1).

The best website about an individual war memorial is probably www.remembering.org.uk, which provides a detailed look at the men who appear on the memorials and roll of honour for Cheltenham. There's even a page about the men who died after the Armistice of wounds contracted during the war but who are not otherwise commemorated.

The website www.burnleyinthegreatwar.info is about Burnley in the war and the men who went away to fight. At the heart are descriptions and information about many of the town's memorials.

Biographies of men on Stockport's war memorial can be found at www.stockport1914-1918.co.uk. There is also a page on war memorials on the Western Front which commemorate those who have no known grave. War memorials of Wolverhampton and district are described at www.warmem.pwp.blueyonder.co.uk.

SCOTTISH WAR MEMORIAL

Scotland's war dead are honoured at the Scots National War Memorial situated in the precincts of Edinburgh Castle (ask for a free pass at the castle's ticket office). The moving Hall of Honour and Shrine was unveiled in 1927 and commemorates the Scottish war effort and in particular the 150,000 Scots who lost their lives in the First World War and 50,000 who did so between 1939 and 1945. If you visit, look out for the small animals hidden among the sculptures! More information

---

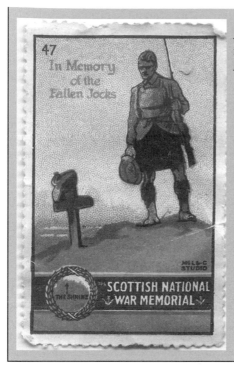

A stamp issued in the early 1920s to raise funds for the Scottish War Memorial. (Author's collection)

can be found at www.snwm.org, where you can also search the Scottish Roll of Honour held at the Memorial. The Roll will tell you the date of a man's death, his unit and service number.

Other Sources

Service records, particularly those for officers, may well include more information about how a man died, correspondence about wills and disposal of personal property. War diaries can also be an invaluable source and may, with a bit of luck, give you some idea of how, when and why a man was killed. The diary for 1/Honourable Artillery Company for 11 October 1916 recorded that 'Pte Freeman A.D. was killed [. . .] his kitten which he carried as a mascot was asleep on his chest, unhurt, when he was found' (WO 95/3118, quoted in James Armstrong, 'The Honourable Artillery Company in the First World War: Sources in the HACArchives', *HAC Journal* (Spring 2002)). Private Freeman is buried at Mailly-Maillet Communal Cemetery Extension.

Newspapers, local and national, published casualty lists. In addition, most local newspapers included short biographies of men from the district who had fallen in action, often with a photograph.

It is possible to obtain an official death certificate, although the information given rarely tells you anything new. The indexes give you the individual's name, regiment, rank and regimental number and the reference number you need to order a certificate. The indexes are available on a number of websites including Findmypast and TheGenealogist. The

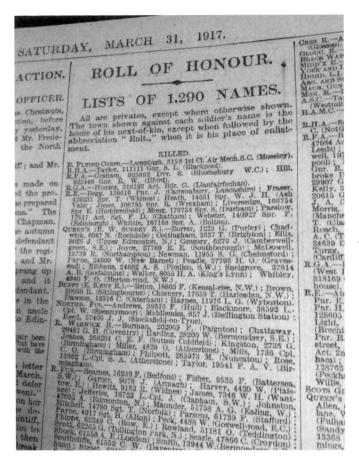

The casualty list from The Times, *31 March 1917. (News International)*

certificate itself will tell you which theatre of operation the individual died in and the reason for death, normally 'killed in action' or 'died of wounds'. Certificates currently cost £9.25 each. There are also separate series for Scottish and Irish servicemen in Edinburgh and Dublin. Those for Scotland are online at www.scotlandspeople.gov.uk. Irish ones are not, so you will need to contact the GROI, Convent Road, Roscommon, Co. Roscommon, www.groireland.ie. Also of interest are Chaplains' Returns and Army Register Books which record births, baptisms, marriages, deaths and burials of soldiers and their families at home and abroad. Indexes are at www.findmypast.co.uk.

Hospital Records

If the service record for your man survives it should contain a Casualty Form (Form B103) which records visits to the doctor, admission to hospital and so on. Of course, many entries are concerned with war-related wounds, but a surprising number of entries refer to normal ailments and complaints. The forms can sometimes be difficult to decode because they also contain details of postings, promotions and demotions, as well as punishments.

The medical sheet for Nurse Ada Laing, VAD. (TNA MH 106/2206)

During the early months of 1916 the Casualty Form for Corporal Theodore Veale VC shows that he had enteritis, influenza, laryngitis (which led to three nights in hospital), debility and trench fever. In fact, most of his file deals with his various medical conditions, including rheumatism which eventually led to his discharge from the Army. However, he does not seem to have been wounded in action.

An efficient system for dealing with casualties was quickly introduced on the outbreak of war to ferry the sick and wounded to the appropriate casualty clearing station or hospital in the rear. A card was compiled for each man, but all these records (with the exception of a small sample) have long been destroyed. The surviving cards are at TNA in series MH 106. There are also admission and discharge registers for six general hospitals, one stationary hospital, six casualty clearing stations, five field ambulances, one ambulance train, one hospital ship and ten medical establishments in Britain. The records are not complete for most of the above and may only cover a very short time span. In addition, there are individual medical records for the officers and men of five units: Leicestershire Regiment; Grenadier Guards; Royal Flying Corps; Royal Field Artillery; and Hussars. There are no indexes and the descriptions in the Catalogue are pretty basic. Even so, if you have time and your ancestor came from one of these units, the records are worth checking out.

In addition, there are boxes of medical records for individual soldiers, as well as nurses and members of Voluntary Aid Detachments (VADs), which cover everything from tonsillitis to trauma, via gunshot wounds and amputation. They can be very detailed. Again they are not indexed, although TNA's Catalogue roughly shows what can be found in each box. You can find out more about these records at www.scarletfinders .co.uk/125.htm.

It may also be worth checking the war diaries of the hospital or casualty clearing station, because occasionally they do record the deaths of patients. No. 2 General Hospital, which was based at Le Havre, includes the names of soldiers who died at the hospital together with their diagnosis, including a number of mental patients, during the first year or so of the war.

If the hospital in Britain to which an ancestor was sent had been a pre-war charity or public hospital, rather than one established in a country house for the duration of the war, it is worth checking the online database of hospital records (www.nationalarchives.gov.uk/hospitalrecords) to see whether anything survives.

An interesting website devoted to the pioneering work of Queen Mary's Hospital, Sidcup in plastic surgery during the war can be found at www.gilliesarchives.org.uk with an index to men helped here on Findmypast. Also worth visiting is www.kentvad.org, which is about nursing in Kent. A list of military hospitals of all kinds established in Britain is at www.1914-1918.net/hospitals_uk.htm.

The most famous hospital opened during the war was the Royal Star & Garter Home which began caring for a few of the most badly injured soldiers, sailors and airmen in 1916. The hospital began life in an old hotel on the top of Richmond Hill in south-west London. The most useful records are patients' registers recording a man's unit, where he was transferred from, the reason for admission and his fate – normally death, but often enough in the early days for insubordination. They are retained by the home and can be consulted by appointment, by contacting the archivist through the website www.starandgarter.org. Some records of the Home are at the Surrey History Centre (www.surreyarchives.org.uk).

Further Reading

Records

It is worth looking out for S B and D B Jarvis, *The Cross of Sacrifice: Officers Who Died in the Service of the British, Indian and East African Regiments and Corps, 1914–1919*, Naval & Military Press, 1993, which combines the information in the Debt of Honour Roll and Soldiers Died in the Great War in alphabetical order.

Chapter 3

ARMY SERVICE RECORDS

I n this chapter we look at the basic records you can use to get a general picture of your ancestors' service. Nearly 6 million men (and 50,000 thousand women) served in the British Army during the First World War and, although some records are missing, you should be able to find something about each of them. However, exactly what cannot be predicted with any certainty. What survives varies greatly, which is one of the great charms of researching the First World War, although it can be frustrating if you find there is very little.

Before you start you need to be reasonably confident of the following about a soldier:

A photograph of my Great-Uncle Private 44405 Henry Philip Stanley Crozier, 18th Battalion King's Royal Rifle Corps. (Adrian Lead)

- Full name.

- The regiment or other unit he served with.

- His service number (if an ordinary soldier or NCO).

Without these details it is very easy to start researching the wrong person.

If you have his medals the information should stamped on the rim or back. Or they may appear on any family papers such as letters and diaries or even written on the back of photographs. Family stories can also help, although often only general statements such as, 'he was at the Battle of the Somme' or 'he was in the trenches when he was buried by an explosion' are obviously not very useful.

You also need to be aware that not

every man served only on the Western Front: he might just as easily have been sent to Gallipoli, the Middle East (Palestine and Mesopotamia), Italy or a number of smaller theatres of operation around the world or even, like my Great-Uncle Stanley, to garrison India. I once had a lengthy email correspondence with a client who did not believe that his great-uncle had not received his Distinguished Conduct Medal on the Western Front, as the family had long believed, but in Palestine. It took a lot of persuasion to make him see the truth!

Medal Index Cards

Every serviceman and woman (as well as a few civilians) who saw service overseas was entitled to two campaign medals, the British War Medal and the Victory Medal. In addition, men who had seen service in France and Flanders between 5 August and midnight 22/23 November 1914 were awarded the 1914 Star (sometimes erroneously called 'The Mons Star') and men who served overseas between 5 August 1914 and 31 December 1915 were entitled to the 1914/15 Star. Each medal was embossed with the man's name and rank and number current at the time of his discharge.

Details of the nearly 5 million men and women to whom these medals were awarded are to be found in medal rolls and on the related medal index cards. They are the most complete listing of individuals who fought in the British Army during the war, containing approximately 90 per cent of soldiers' names.

These cards provided an index to the rolls and were also used by the

Examples of the British War and Allied Victory medals given to all British and Dominion forces who served overseas. (Author's collection)

workers in Woolwich Dockyard who stamped the medals with the individual's name. Occasionally, you may come across a manuscript cross-marked by the rank or service number to show the engraver the number and rank to be used.

The great advantage with these cards is that they list everyone who was

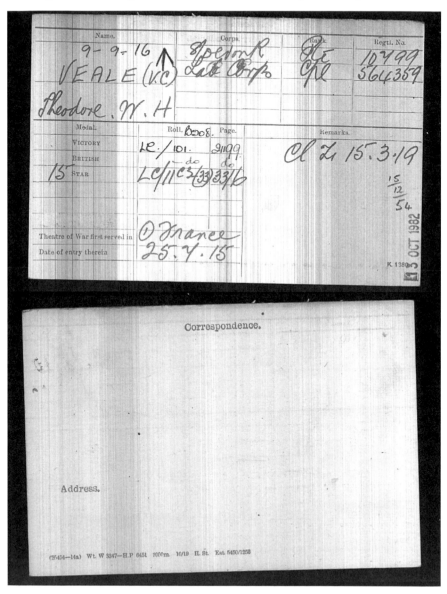

The unusually complete medal index card for Theodore Veale VC.
(Ancestry/TNA WO 372)

entitled to a medal, which is doubly helpful if the service record you are looking for has been destroyed.

There are in fact several designs, but regardless of which one you come across they should tell you:

- The rank he held at the end of his service.

- Regimental numbers (other ranks only).

- Units served in.

- The actual medals to which he was entitled together with the place on the medal roll where they are to be found.

- The date he went overseas (if it was before the end of 1915).

- The theatre of war in which he served. If it was the Western Front, it might be abbreviated as being F&F for 'France and Flanders' or the number 1 or 1A. A full list is given on the appropriate webpage in the Online Record Services section of TNA's website.

In addition, there may be extra information, such as:

- The date of discharge or when he was killed in action.

- A note of gallantry medals a man was awarded.

- A note that he was entitled to wear the oak-leaf emblem on the Victory Medal for being Mentioned in Despatches (MiD), usually abbreviated to EMB.

- A note that he was entitled to wear a clasp (actually a silver rose) on his 1914 Star, which indicates that he had served within the sound of enemy guns, usually indicated by the word clasp. Individuals had to apply for the clasp after the war, so many did not bother.

The cards are available online at both Ancestry (who call them 'British Army WWI Medal Rolls Index Cards') and through TNA's Online Records Service. Of the two, Ancestry offers by far the better reproduction in colour and provides both sides of each card, which occasionally includes the address to which the medals were sent. Officers' addresses in particular can be given and there may be a note that the medals were returned for some reason. The Online Records Service, however, includes cards for women and civilians. The indexing is also better, allowing you to search by forename, service number or unit. This can be surprisingly useful if you are unsure of an individual's details.

With these cards it is possible to track the individual in the medal rolls themselves, which are at TNA in series WO 329 (see below).

There were two other campaign medals available. The Territorial Force War Medal was awarded to men who were members of the Territorial Forces at the beginning of the war and who saw service overseas, but were not eligible for the 1914 or 1914/15 Stars. This is a rare medal as only 34,000 were issued.

Much more common was the Silver War Badge: a small, circular label badge made of sterling silver, which bore the king's initials, a crown and the inscriptions 'For King and Empire' and 'Services Rendered'. The badge was authorised in 1916 in order to provide former soldiers with some type of identification to show that they had faithfully served king and country. Half of the 2 million or so military personnel discharged from the armed forces (Navy and RAF as well as the Army) during the war for illness or injury, including those who left the services before the award was instituted in 1916, applied to wear the badge. The fact that a man received the badge may sometimes be noted on his medal index card. In addition, there are special distinctive cards for men who were issued the Silver War Badge, and these can be found with the other cards in the normal way. They are not very informative, but may give you the date of enlistment and discharge and the cause of discharge.

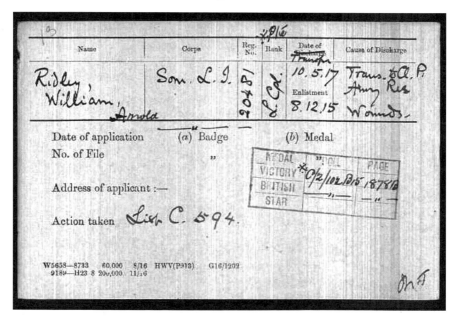

The index card for the Silver War Badge for the actor William Arnold Ridley, who played Private Godfrey in the long-running BBC show Dad's Army. *(Ancestry/TNA WO 372)*

Regtl. No.	Rank	Name (in full)		Unit discharged from which Transferred to Class P army Reserve	No. of Badge and Certificate (To be completed at War Office)	Date of :— Enlistment	Discharge	Cause of Discharge Transfer (Wounds or Sickness and para. of K.R.)		Whether served Overseas (Yes or No)	Whether awarded a Pension or Gratuity
16291	Private	Clarke	Edward	Somerset L.I	181579	16-11-14	19-2-17	Wounds	To Class P	Yes	yes
16525	Private	Flynn	Andrew	-do-	181600	28-11-14	644-16	Wounds	-do-	Yes	yes
16810	Private	Trapnell	Frank	-do-	181601	31-12-14	4-2-17	Wounds	-do-	Yes	yes
17069	Private	Stepney	Alfred George	-do-	181602	19-1-15	15-2-17	Wounds	-do-	Yes	yes
17271	Private	Pace	George	-do-	181603	8-9-14	17-9-17	Sickness	-do-	Yes	yes
17289	Private	Nurton	Francis Geo:	-do-	181604	15-2-15	29-1-17	Wounds	-do-	Yes	yes
17378	Private	Collacot	Richard Geo:	-do-	181605	24-2-15	4-2-17	Wounds	-do-	Yes	yes
20456	Private	Taylor	Percy F.P	-do-	181606	22-11-15	24-3-17	Wounds	-do-	Yes	yes
20481	L/Corpl	Ridley	William.A	-do-	18160?	8-12-15	10-5-17	Wounds	-do-	Yes	yes
21481	Private	Harwood	Stanley C	-do-	181608	15-11-15	14-4-17	Wounds	-do-	Yes	yes
21684	Private	Whatley	Augustus	-do-	181609	24-3-16	13-4-17	Wounds	-do-	Yes	yes
26955	Private	Marshall	Stanley	-do-	181610	22-2-16	13-2-17	Wounds	-do-	Yes	yes

I certify that the particulars furnished hereon are correct.

Place EXETER.   Date 5 - MAY 1917

To Charge of Records, N? 8 District
Signature and Rank of Officer certifying Claimants' service.

I certify that Badges and Certificates, numbered as above, have been issued to the individuals concerned.

Place EXETER.   Date 10 MAY 1917

To Charge of Records, N? 8 District
Signature and Rank of Officer certifying issue.

The entry in the medal roll of the Silver War Badge for William Arnold Ridley. (Ancestry/TNA WO 372)

Ancestry has digitised the rolls listing all the men who received the Silver War Badge. The records will tell you the individual's name, rank, regimental number, unit, dates of enlistment and discharge, and, most importantly, reason for discharge. In most cases this is a fairly bald statement, such as 'sick' or 'wounds', and a reference to the appropriate King's Regulation. Sometimes you will find entries for men discharged because they were over age.

Very occasionally you may come across a card stamped with details of medals awarded for service in colonial skirmishes which had nothing directly to do with the First World War itself, such as the Khedive's Service Medal (sometimes called the Sultan's Service Medal) for service in Sudan or Indian General Service Medal which relates to service in the 3rd Afghan War in 1919–20 along the North West Frontier. If this is the case, you can find slightly more information in Ancestry's set of Army medal rolls (known as UK Military Campaign Medal and Award Rolls, 1793–1949).

Can't Find Your Man?

The medal index cards are pretty easy to use, but occasionally you may come unstuck. Here is a list of things to check:

- No campaign medals were issued to men who were based solely in Britain (including Ireland). However, a number of men who never served overseas for one reason or another received the Silver War Badge, so it may be worth searching the appropriate database on Ancestry. Noël Coward, for example, was called up to the Artists' Rifles in March 1918. However, doctors described him as 'suffering from headaches and general nervous disability' and he lasted only 158 days before being discharged. He received the Silver War Badge despite getting no further to the Western Front than a military hospital in Colchester.

- While soldiers were sent their campaign medals automatically, officers had to apply for theirs and not all did.

- Men who were sent overseas for the first time after 11 November 1918 were not entitled to war medals.

- Clerks must occasionally have made mistakes in the spelling of names, so it is worth checking common surname variants, for example, Pyke for Pike, Clarke for Clark, etc. And for many men, including my Great-Uncle Stanley Crozier, only their initials were used (in his case H P S Crozier, for Henry Philip Stanley). It does not help that the Ancestry search engine automatically lumps surname variants together.

If you can't find your man on Ancestry it is worth checking TNA's set as the record sets are not quite the same. In addition, TNA's indexing is superior.

MEDAL ROLLS

The cards are actually an index to a voluminous set of medal rolls, which are in series WO 329 at TNA. The numbers of the cards will lead you to the exact volume and page. However, as the handwriting is not always clear it can be a slightly tricky process. With one exception, the rolls will not tell you anything that is not already available on the cards, although occasionally clerks note the death of a man or other information. I once came across a note for a man who was shot for desertion.

However, these rolls are useful because they will tell you the battalion a man was in at the time of his discharge. From this you can find the appropriate battalion war diary. Frustratingly, this only works for infantry regiments.

Service Records – Other Ranks and Non-commissioned Officers

If you are lucky you may find a service record for your man. There's some good news and bad news here. The good is news is that almost all surviving records are available on Ancestry (the exceptions are described below). The bad news is that less than two records in five survive. The remainder were destroyed in a fire in 1940.

Surviving records may include the papers of:

- Soldiers discharged between 1914 and 1920.

- Soldiers killed in action between 1914 and 1920.

- Soldiers who served in the war and died of wounds or disease without being discharged to pension.

- Soldiers who were demobilised at the end of the war.

At first glance there seems to be no pattern as to what survives and what has been lost. However, it is as well to be aware of the following:

- If your ancestor was killed in action, there is less likely to be a file for him, partly because the records were largely kept for pension purposes. Certainly there is no record for Stanley Crozier who was killed in October 1918 having served throughout the war, whereas there is one for his younger brother Basil who survived the war, having been called up on his 17th birthday earlier in 1918.

- A higher proportion of files than might be expected survive for men, like Fred Wilkinson and Theodore Veale VC, who were transferred to the Labour Corps because they were no longer fit for service at the front.

- Files seem to survive for men who served in the Honourable Artillery Company (HAC).

- There seem to be relatively few service records for men in Irish regiments.

There are in fact two series of files that you may need to consult:

- WO 363, sometimes known as the 'burnt' records as they were damaged in some way by fire or water in 1940. The originals were in a very fragile condition, which is why the decision was taken to film them. They are for men who were killed in action, died of wounds or disease without being discharged to service, or demobilised at the end of the war.

Ancestry refers to these records as being 'British Army WWI Service Records, 1914–1920'.

- WO 364, sometimes referred to as the 'unburnt' records because they were either untouched by the fire or subsequently added from other sources. These generally relate to the discharge of regular soldiers at the end of their period of service. These records are unlikely to contain individuals who did not claim a pension or be about soldiers who were killed in action and had no dependants (as there would have been no one to claim a pension). Nor are they likely to contain documents on soldiers who were discharged from demobilisation at the end of the war and did not claim a pension (since they were generally not eligible for one). The series also covers soldiers discharged on medical and associated grounds, including those who died after the award of a pension.

Ancestry refers to these records as being 'British Army WWI Pension Records, 1914–1920'.

In practice, you may need to search both series before you find your man. It helps if you know in which unit a man served and his regimental number, particularly for men with common names.

Individual files contain a wide range of paperwork, which can be informative if at times a little bewildering, particularly if you are unfamiliar with how the Army of the period operated. A further problem is that many documents are filed out of order. And it does not help that on occasion stray documents often appear in the middle of totally unrelated files.

In addition, many papers can be difficult to read as they were either burnt or they suffered from water damage as the fireman tried to control the fire in the file store. However, the quality of the microfilming is good and the quality of the online images is excellent.

With a little practice and patience you should be able to decipher the forms and build up an intimate portrait of the individual. The forms certainly repay close study.

No two files are the same. Some are very detailed with a variety of forms, letters and other paperwork, but in other cases you may only find a man's attestation form or perhaps a medical record. This often seems to be the case for men whose service for one reason or another was fairly brief or never took them overseas. For example, the actor Basil Rathbone's record only includes the attestation form into the 14th Reserve Battalion, London Regiment and an incomplete form about his discharge. However, in this case the reason may well be that Rathbone was subsequently commissioned from the ranks into the Liverpool Scottish.

Of particular importance is the attestation form which was completed by the individual on enlistment. This will indicate when and where a man enlisted and was discharged and give other personal details such as civilian occupation, home address and date of birth. My Great-Uncle Walter Basil Crozier, Guards Machine Gun Regiment, was noted as being a 'music hall artiste'. More prosaically, when he enlisted Walter Pye, Durham Light Infantry, was a 'butcher'. There may also be a physical description. Fred Wilkinson had a tattoo of crossed flags on his right arm.

If a man was a pre-war regular soldier, a part-time member of the Territorial Army or had been recalled to the colours, then the file will include his pre-war attestation form (and details of his pre-war service) which might occasionally go back to the Boer War or earlier. Aged 19, Fred Wilkinson, for example, enlisted into the Buffs (East Kent Regiment) in February 1907. He had been a farm labourer and enlisted to escape grinding poverty at home. He had previously tried to join the Grenadier Guards, but was not quite tall enough.

The attestation form is usually the first or second form to appear in a service record and is present in all but a small number of service records.

The other form to look out for is Form B103/1 'Casualty Form – Active Service'. Despite the name it includes far more than wounds and hospital stays. It may provide the following information:

- Promotions through the ranks (and demotions if appropriate).

- Details of the units he served in.

- When he went overseas and often when he returned to Britain to be discharged.

- Details of medical treatments received. The record for Walter Basil Crozier, for example, notes he received contusion of the right eye during training and later in 1918 he was hospitalised with appendicitis. And for Fred Wilkinson that he had had malaria, which prevented him being sent with his battalion to Salonika where malaria was prevalent. Theodore Veale seems to have been a regular visitor to the doctor, but, for some psychological reasons, his medical record improved after he was awarded the Victoria Cross during the summer of 1916.

- Notes of disciplinary offences.

- Date and reason for death. Walter Pye was noted as being 'killed in action' on 4 October 1918.

Another interesting form is the Regimental Conduct Sheet, which notes disciplinary offences. Soldiers during the First World War in general were surprisingly well behaved. Most appearances before courts martial concerned drunkenness or petty theft, but occasionally there are more interesting offences. Walter Pye, who seems to have found it difficult to adjust to Army discipline, was confined to barracks for five days for 'having a dirty rifle while on guard duty' and received 96 hours' detention for 'creating a disturbance in Paragon station'.

If a man died during his Army service there may well be correspondence about his will and personal effects, as well as perhaps letters from the next of kin seeking more information about the circumstances of the loss of their man.

What the records will not do is to tell you very much about any fighting he was engaged in, any gallantry medals awarded (with the exception of the Victoria Cross) or give you any real idea of his life in the Army. However, you can use the war diaries to obtain this information.

These service records are online at www.ancestry.co.uk/military. For some records every page has been filmed several times, so it can be a little tedious going through an individual's file.

The 'burnt' documents in WO 363 (but not the pension documents in WO 364) are also available on microfilm from the Family History Library in Salt Lake City through local Family History Centres. If you want to use the records in this way, ask for 'Military records of the British Army, 1914–1920'. Details of local centres can be found at www.familysearch.org. The films are arranged in strict alphabetical order by surname and then by forenames.

Alternatives

If you can't find your man in these records, there are other places to look:

- Records for soldiers and NCOs of the Household Cavalry (which include the Life Guards, Royal Horse Guards and Household Battalion) are not with the other service records. They are online at the Online Records Service with the originals at TNA in WO 400.

- The Guards still keep their own records (see below).

- If a soldier was eventually commissioned as an officer, some basic records relating to his time as a private (generally the attestation documents completed when a man joined up) should be with his officer records.

- If a man transferred to either the RN or (from 1918) RAF, his service record went with him.

- If he continued to serve after 1920, his service record is still with the MoD (see below).

- Men who served overseas were entitled to campaign medals and there will be a medal index card, which can provide basic information (see above).

ARMY SERVICE NUMBERS (REGIMENTAL NUMBERS)

Each ordinary soldier and NCO was given a regimental number when he enlisted. It was one of the ways he was identified in documents and on his identity tag if he was killed in action. Even today it helps considerably if you know your ancestors' service numbers, particularly if you are researching men with common names. And, where search engines allow it, you can either search by it or use it as a key word to make searching easier.

Until 1920 each regiment maintained its own system of numbering. When a man changed regiment, as became increasingly common during the First World War, he was issued a new service number which bore no resemblance to his old one. Fred Wilkinson of The Buffs was assigned the number 8434 when he enlisted in 1907. When he was transferred to the Labour Corps to guard prisoners of war in December 1918 he became 443706 Private Fred Wilkinson.

And, of course, the same number would be given to totally different men in different regiments. For example, there was 51306 Private Joe Harrison in the West Yorkshire Regiment and 51306 Private George Millichip in the Machine Gun Corps and thirty-one other men with the same number scattered across the Army.

As a rough guide the lower his number the earlier a man enlisted. Men who had been pre-war regulars might have very low numbers indeed (a revised system had been introduced in 1882). Very occasionally you may come across recruitment registers in regimental museums which list recruits in regimental number order. Findmypast has an example for part of Surrey.

In addition, regimental headquarters introduced a number of different prefixes to help differentiate the flood of new recruits in 1914 and later. The most common letter was G which stood for General Service (i.e., for the duration of the war), followed by T for temporary or Territorial Army. A list of prefixes can be found at http://www.1914-1918.net/prefixes.html.

It was not until 1920 that Army numbers, as opposed to regimental or service numbers, were introduced. They were allocated to a soldier on enlistment which he kept throughout his career, no matter how many times he changed his unit. The man who was assigned Army number 1 was Regimental Sergeant Major George James Redman of the Royal Army Service Corps. He had enlisted in the Corps aged 14 in 1888, later seeing service in South Africa and during the First World War. There is a medal index card which shows his old number. He was discharged shortly after receiving his new number. Incidentally, officers at this time were not given numbers.

It can be difficult to find a service number. You may find it on any medals, letters and diaries you may have inherited. Otherwise it can be found on the medal index cards or, if he was killed in action, in CWGC records. Remember that it in almost all cases it was the final number that a man was assigned which will be engraved on his medal or appear in CWGC records.

THE GUARDS

Everything you have read about service records does not apply to men and officers who served in one of the five guards regiments (that is the Coldstream, Grenadiers, Irish, Scottish and Welsh Guards). Unlike the other regiments, they still keep their own service records. Therefore, if you are researching an ancestor who was a Guardsman you will need to contact the appropriate regimental headquarters at Wellington Barracks, Birdcage Walk, London SW1E 6HQ. You will need to specify which regiment you are writing to. Some regiments require payment for supplying a copy, others invite a donation. In all cases you should at first write, asking for the form that the regimental archivist needs to carry out a search.

However, it is still worth checking the ordinary service records because it is not unknown for records of individual guardsmen to turn up here. Certainly, Ancestry has a record for my Great-Uncle Walter Basil Crozier who served in the Guards Machine Gun Regiment in late 1918.

The Guards Museum may also have additional information, such as photographs, but at the time of writing their website (www.theguardsmuseum.com) is not particularly forthcoming about what exactly the collections contain. However, you may have more success if you write to The Guards Museum, Wellington Barracks, Birdcage Walk, London SW1E 6HQ. But remember as the website tersely says, the museum does not have any service records.

Service Records – Officers

Surviving service records are at TNA in two series:

- WO 339 – records and correspondence for Regular Army and Emergency Reserve officers. (There is an index in WO 338.)

- WO 374 – Territorial Army officers, officers who came out of retirement and other officers recruited because of their skills in civilian life (such as railway managers).

In practice there seems to be little difference between the two series, so if you can't find a man in one series you should check the other.

It is estimated that about 15 per cent of records no longer survive. In particular, there are known gaps for men who reached the rank of colonel or above or were temporary officers in the RAMC. In such cases it is probably worth approaching the regimental museum to see whether they can help.

It can be fairly easy to find records because there is just one file for each officer. These are listed in the Catalogue. In WO 339 some entries in the Catalogue include the individual's full name and regiment, and in WO 374 there is often an indication of the final rank an officer held, but if you are researching a common name you might have to order a number of files to find the man you want. Generally, the lower the piece number the earlier a man became an officer, which can be useful if you are not sure which file to start with.

At some stage the records were weeded and much material was destroyed. Records for men who survived are generally less full than those who died in action. Basil Rathbone's record contains only his attestation papers joining the Army as a private, his application to become an officer in 1916 and reports from a medical board which met to consider an attack of measles (TNA WO 374/56295).

Even so, there may be correspondence concerning money, length of service and pensions rather than about an individual's war service. Occasionally there is correspondence about post-war employment. And a surprising number of former officers seemed to have got into trouble with the authorities, often regarding cheques that bounced.

If an officer came through the ranks, then there should be his original enlistment document and recommendations from the commanding officer. These are worth looking at closely because they can contain personal details which would otherwise be missing. They usually contain a physical description. For both Basil Rathbone and Eric Roper, for example, they contain physical descriptions (both were over 6ft 2in tall), the date and place of their marriages and pre-war military service (Rathbone had been in the Office Training Corps at Repton School, and Roper was a member of one of Devon's territorial units).

Occasionally there may be additional correspondence. Perhaps none was so fulsome as for the writer and apiarist Tickner Edwardes, who had

Attestation document for Eric Roper. (TNA WO 339/65178)

been a sergeant in the RAMC and was now an officer cadet, by Courtenay Shaw, the commanding officer of his Officer Training Battalion in the Labour Corps. Edwardes, Shaw wrote, is:

> about 50 years old . . . one of our leading authorities on bee culture. He has a son in the RA . . . he is through and through a 'Sahib' and very fine young old boy. As his experience has been entirely in the RAMC he wants if possible not to sever his connections with that corps of whose record he is extraordinarily proud. He believes that it is possible to obtain a commission in it although he is not a medico, if he can get his name and record put before the right people . . . he joined the cadet company in Cambridge which I commanded in October last and stuck to the training alongside of the young men, he was never sick or sorry and although past the time for taking an

active part in the athletics of the company he took a leading part on the general life of the company. I feel sure that he would justify himself in an administrative capacity in the RAMC, if he could get a commission in it . . . he is the right type. (WO 374/22040)

Tickner had his wish and was assigned to a RAMC pathology laboratory which investigated cures for malaria.

There may on occasion be more personal material. The file for 2/Lieutenant J B Priestley includes several letters written to the War Office about his being unable to return to his unit because he was sick, and Lieutenant Siegfried Sassoon's file has papers about his pacifist *Declaration Against the War*, which was published in June 1917.

Some of the fullest records are likely to relate to appearances before medical boards, where they might well be the proceedings of the boards, details of railway warrants issued so that the man could attend them and related paperwork. For Lieutenant Henry Pillow, Middlesex Regiment,

Copy of the description of the funeral of Lieutenant Eric Roper MC which was sent to his widow after his death in 1916. (TNA WO 339/65178)

55

there are claims for taxis across London and railway journeys from Egypt back to East Anglia, where he was to be trained as a pilot. In the case of 2/Lieutenant John Dunn, 4th King's Own Scottish Borderers, a medical board in April 1916 found that he contracted dysentery and malaria on active service and that 'he is still far from being well. His bowels are very irregular, sometimes he has three, and sometimes four motions a day. He has lost weight and is much exhausted after a walk of a couple of miles.' (WO 374/21319). He had been a regular soldier prior to the war before being commissioned into the Territorials in early 1915. Dunn does not seem to have returned to active service or returned to full health, but was transferred to the Labour Corps to command an Agricultural Company in Dumfriesshire.

If a man died during his service, there are likely to be papers relating to the administration of his will and dispersal of his effects. In addition, there may be correspondence with the next of kin who were often trying to find out the circumstances of their son, brother or husband's death. For Lieutenant Eric Roper there is an unusually detailed account of his wounds and funeral: 'Lt and Adjutant E Roper, 17th battalion Royal Fusilliers, died from gunshot wounds head (compound fracture skull) arm and forearm (right) and leg (right), 12th of September. Interred in Govin Cemetery . . . on 13th September 1916. The chaplain officiating at the burial was Revd W.H. Brown, Chaplain to the Forces.' (WO 339/65178).

For Lieutenant Henry Pillow (WO 339/58909) there is a copy of a memorial card that his grieving mother had had printed which contained extracts from letters from his commanding officer and comrades in 7 Squadron RFC.

> He was just the right type, very modest and unassuming, very keen on his job, very quiet about it, yet one who would successfully carry out whatever he was given to do. His loss is one which I regret deeply. He was the sort whose example is infectious – which is the thing we value most highly, in proportion it is most rare.

For men who died in action there is often a list of possessions which were returned to the next of kin. Even after nearly a century they can bring a lump to the throat. For Lieutenant Roper they included a range of smoking materials, including pipes, cigarette cases, a meerschaum cigarette holder, safety razor and eleven blades, and a collapsible drinking cup. And for Lieutenant Pillow there was a crucifix and medallion, his aviator's certificate, a penknife with chain (broken) and key register ticket, papers and snapshots, etc.

At the time of writing, the records are not yet online and you will need to consult the original files at TNA.

ARMY LISTS AND THE *LONDON GAZETTE*

Officers are listed in the Army Lists. These are an easy way to confirm whether an ancestor was an officer, because the Lists include everyone who was commissioned. They will tell you which regiment or unit he was with, his rank and if he had been promoted to it.

In fact, there are two series of Army Lists: monthly and quarterly. The monthly Lists record everybody by regiment (with a detailed index). Often there will be additional abbreviations by a name which will tell you that he was in the Territorial Force or had attended specific levels of proficiency. Quarterly Lists (published every January, April, July and October) are arranged by individual with details of his promotions. A symbol of crossed swords by an individual's name indicates war service.

TNA has a complete set on the shelves in the Open Reading Room, and copies can be found at the IWM, NAM and some regimental museums. TheGenealogist (www.thegenealogist.co.uk) provides a small selection of Army Lists to subscribers.

Much the same information can be found in the *London Gazette*, which because it is online is much easier to use. The oldest daily paper in Britain, the *London Gazette* has been published by the government since November 1665. Initially it contained news stories, including accounts of the Great Fire of London, and classified advertising but it has long been the British Government's official gazette.

The term 'gazetted' refers to the announcement of a promotion or a gallantry medal. In particular promotions took effect from the day of their publication. Occasionally you may come across correspondence about this in Army officers' files. Hard-up men could get quite desperate if there was a delay in gazetting a promotion. On 22 March 1919, Lieutenant Tickner Edwardes, RAMC, wrote to his former commanding officer, Captain Angus Macdonald, that he was 'greatly concerned' that he had not been gazetted a captain: 'Do jog the powers for me. You (and [Col] Sir Ronald [Ross]) led me to believe that I had done rather creditably at the bug-killing game. But deep misgivings are beginning to assail me on this head owing to silence of Gazette.' (TNA WO 374/22040). Eventually, the promotion appeared in the *Gazette* on 3 April.

For family historians the *London Gazette* is an important source for the following information:

- Appointments – it prints details of the appointment and promotion of officers in the services (including those in the reserve forces and Dominion services). The surnames and initials of individual officers are given, together with the regiment, ship or unit to which they

8980 SUPPLEMENT to the LONDON GAZETTE, 13 SEPTEMBER, 1916.

rank of Capt., with precedence as from the 28th June 1915, on alteration in posting. 5th Aug. 1916.

2nd Lt. (temp. Capt.) H. C. Ashenden to be Adjt., vice 2nd Lt. (temp. Lt.) H. W. Skinner. 5th Aug. 1916.

Northumbrian Brigade.—Capt. (temp. Maj.) J. W. Merryweather relinquishes his temp. rank on alteration in posting. 25th Aug. 1916.

Wessex Brigade.—2nd Lt. (temp. Lt.) P. J. Cole relinquishes his temp. rank on alteration in posting. 15th Aug. 1916.

2nd Lt. Q. E. M. A. King to be temp. Lt. 14th Sept. 1916.

ROYAL GARRISON ARTILLERY.

Hampshire.—2nd Lt. (temp. Lt.) R. Sherlock is seconded for duty with Anti Aircraft Brigade. 14th Sept. 1916.

Kent.—2nd Lt. R. F. E. Whittaker to be temp. Lt. 24th May 1916.

2nd Lt. (temp. Lt.) R. F. E. Whittaker is seconded for duty with Anti Aircraft Battery. 24th May 1916.

ROYAL ENGINEERS.

East Lancashire Divisional Engineers.—2nd Lt. (temp. Lt.) Clyde Higgs, from Divisional Signal Company, to be 2nd Lt., with precedence from 9th Sept. 1915. 14th Sept. 1916.

2nd Lt. Clyde Higgs to be temp. Lt., with precedence from 30th Jan. 1916. 14th Sept. 1916.

Devon Fortress Engineers.—Lt. (temp. Capt.) G. L. Appleton relinquishes his commission in order to take up a cadetship at the Royal Military Academy. 7th Sept. 1916.

Renfrewshire Fortress Engineers, Field Company.—2nd Lt. (temp. Lt.) William Moon, from a Cyclist Bn., to be 2nd Lt., with precedence from 14th Nov. 1914. 21st Aug. 1916.

INFANTRY.

The Royal Scots.—2nd Lt. R. Waugh relinquishes his commission. 14th Sept. 1916.

Royal Lancaster Regiment.—The undermentioned Cadets, from Artists Rifles O.T.C., to be 2nd Lts. (on prob.). 5th Sept. 1916 :—

Edward Charles Whitworth.
James Stuart Paterson.
Sidney William Foxon.
Lindon Rayner Keighley.
George Arthur Taylor.

Cadet Clement William Ford, from the Artists Rifles O.T.C., to be 2nd Lt. (on prob.). 5th Sept. 1916.

Northumberland Fus.—Lt. (temp. Capt.) W. N. Craigs relinquishes the temp. rank of Capt., with precedence as from 22nd Aug. 1914, and is seconded for duty with the Machine Gun Corps. 4th Sept. 1916.

Liverpool Regt.—The following announcement is substituted for that which appeared in the Gazette of the 24th Jan. 1916 :—

2nd Lt. J. E. Redding to be temp. Capt., with precedence as from 11th Sept. 1915. 22nd Dec. 1915.

Norfolk Regt.—Cadet Lewis Lawrence Johnson to be 2nd Lt. (on prob.). 5th Sept. 1916.

Lincolnshire Regt.—Cadet Francis Charles Evison, from Artists Rifles O.T.C., to be 2nd Lt. (on prob.). 5th Sept. 1916.

Leicestershire Regt.—Cadet Francis William Willett, from Artists Rifles O.T.C., to be 2nd Lt. (on prob.). 5th Sept. 1916.

Cadet Leslie Trevor Franklin, from the Inns of Court O.T.C., to be 2nd Lt. (on prob.). 5th Sept. 1916.

Gloucestershire Regt.—The undermentioned Cadets, from Artists Rifles O.T.C., to be 2nd Lts. (on prob.). 5th Sept. 1916 :—

Wilfred Joseph Dutton.
Arthur Alexander Crowe.
John Alfred Beavon.
Alfred George Beadell.
George Howard Wintle.
Rowland Kitchiner Walter.
Martin Mark Stanley Lemon.
Josiah Weldon Sleap.
Robert William Edwin Bunn.
Percival Arthur Cleaver.
James Bertram Tebb.
Herbert Thomas Harold Painter.
George Francis Shute.
Cadet Ian MacLellan Turner Wilson, from the Artists Rifles O.T.C., to be 2nd Lt. (on prob.). 5th Sept. 1916.

South Lancashire Regt.—Cadet Arthur James Lines, from the Artists Rifles O.T.C., to be 2nd Lt. (on prob.). 5th Sept. 1916.

Oxfordshire and Buckinghamshire L.I.—The undermentioned Cadets, from Artists Rifles O.T.C., to be 2nd Lts. (on prob.). 5th Sept. 1916.—

Reginald Thomas.
Ebenezer Frederick King.
Alfred Thomas Adams Wilkins.
Frank Perceval Taylor.
Leonard Maurice Brettelle.
William Rey Gill.
Edwin Henry Fawcett.
Raymond Elder Norman.
Basil Coutts Carr Olivier.
Joseph Henry Piperno.
Douglas Gerald Rydings.
Frederick Villiers Tuthill.
Basil Vokes.

Essex Regt.—Cadet Alfred John Parfitt, from Artists Rifles O.T.C., to be 2nd Lt. (on prob.). 5th Sept. 1916.

. The undermentioned Cadets, from Artists Rifles O.T.C., to be 2nd Lts. (on prob.). 5th Sept. 1916 :—

Alfred Vernon Hughes.
William John Tweddle.
Leslie Charles Cunningham.

Manchester Regt.—2nd Lt. E. J. Agelasto relinquishes his commission on account of ill-health. 14th Sept. 1916.

Highland L.I.—2nd Lt. (temp. Lt.) T. B. Forrest is now seconded for duty with a Machine Gun Coy. 16th Mar. 1916.

Seaforth Highlanders.—The undermentioned Cadets to be 2nd Lts. (on prob.). 5th Sept. 1916 :—

Eric Urquhart Neale-Smith.
Charles Alexander Webster.
James Spence.

Gordon Highlanders.—Cadet John James Chalmers to be 2nd Lt. (on prob.). 5th Sept. 1916.

A page from the London Gazette, *13 September 1916 with details of the promotion and appointment of officers. (The Stationery Office/London Gazette)*

belong, and the date the promotion (even temporary ones) took place. Inevitably, publication may be months after the event took place, but it will always give the date the promotion was granted. Entries also include details of where officers were assigned after leaving Officer Training Corps or where individuals resign their commissions because of ill-health or for other reasons. A brief summary of the reason for their resignation is often given.

- Medals – the *London Gazette* includes details of the award of gallantry medals to both officers and other ranks (such as the Victoria Cross, George Cross, Distinguished Service Cross or Military Medal). Occasionally a citation is included explaining in general terms how the medal was won. One is always given for the Victoria Cross. The citation for Jack Cornwell, 'the Boy VC', who won Britain's highest gallantry at the Battle of Jutland reads:

The King has been graciously pleased to approve the grant of the Victoria Cross to Boy, First Class, John Travers Cornwell, O.N. J.42563 (died 2nd June, 1916), for the conspicuous act of bravery specified below.

Mortally wounded early in the action, Boy, First Class, John Travers Cornwell remained standing alone at a most exposed post, quietly awaiting orders, until the end of the action, with the gun's crew dead and wounded all round him. His age was under sixteen and a half years. (*London Gazette*, 15 September 1916, issue 19752, p. 9085)

The individual's full name is given, together with regiment, ship or unit, rank and where appropriate service number.

- Despatches – accounts of battles, campaigns and wars written by the commander-in-chief. They would usually include the names of those officers and ratings who the commander particularly thought worthy of mention. The practice of including names had largely been dropped by the First World War, but a Mention in Despatches remained the lowest form of gallantry award (as it does today). Men so honoured where entitled to wear a silver oak leaf on the Victory Medal.

The *London Gazette* has been digitised and is online at www.london-gazette.co.uk. In theory, it is fully searchable but the indexing is very erratic, so you may need to hunt down a set of the originals to double check (sets are at TNA and BL). One tip is, if you have a service number search using this rather than the name of the individual as the search engine is better at recognising numbers than words.

Despite the problems with indexing, the *Gazette* is a very useful resource, particularly if you are researching officers or winners of gallantry medals.

Alternatives

If you can't find a record for an officer here are a few tips about what to do next:

- Records of Guards officers are still with the regimental archives (see above).

- Service files for a few notable individuals, including Field Marshal Lord Haig and the poet Wilfred Owen, are in series WO 138. In addition, WO 340 contains a selection of registers of correspondence with officers.

- Biographical details of officers in the Army Medical Corps are listed in Sir William Macarlane's *A List of Commissioned Medical Officers of the Army, 1660–1960* (Wellcome Library, 1968). However, it does not include officers who were on temporary or wartime commissions, like Tickner Edwardes. Both TNA and SOG have copies.

SERVICE RECORDS AFTER 1920

Although the British Army contracted rapidly after the Armistice in 1918, a number of men chose to make it their career.

If your ancestor continued to serve in the Army after the end of 1920 (for officers the cut-off period is April 1922), his service record will be with the MOD. It is unlikely that these service records will be transferred to TNA for a decade or more. So far as is known these records are complete.

They are accessible either to the individual themselves or to the next of kin only, unless the man died more than twenty-five years ago. You may have to prove that you are the closest surviving relation. In addition, there could be a charge, currently £30, for a search. Because of other more pressing demands on the staff it may take up to a year for you to receive your forebear's file.

You need to write to the Army Personnel Centre, Historic Disclosures, Mailpoint 400, Kentigern House, 65 Brown Street, Glasgow G2 8EX. Full details, including a form that has to be completed, is available on the Service Personnel and Veterans Agency website at www.veterans-uk.info. There is also a helpline, 0800 169 2277.

More information can be found in a NAM Information Leaflet (No. 4), *Soldiers Records Post 1920*, from their website at www.nam.ac.uk/sites/default/files/research-information-4.pdf.

Alternatives

- Many veterans served in the Home Guard during the Second World War. Home Guard service records will be transferred to TNA within the next few years. Those for County Durham are already available on TNA's Online Records Service. The information contained in these records is disappointing and generally only relates to promotions within the Home Guard or minor medical conditions.

- Regimental archives may also have information about an ancestor's subsequent career in the Army, particularly if he was an officer.

- You can carry on tracing an officer's career through the Army Lists, which continue to be published after the First World War. In addition, promotions, resignations and changes of regiment were also published in the War Office sections of the *London Gazette*. The *Gazette* will also tell you if a man transferred between regiments or even, on occasion, between services. Lieutenant Edward Norman Tickner Edwardes, Royal Field Artillery, for example, is noted as being seconded to the RAF on 14 October 1921 (and his subsequent death in what may have been an air accident is listed in 1928).

- It is unlikely, however, that you will be able to find much about ordinary soldiers, although the retirement of long-serving men is likely to be marked in regimental magazines where they exist.

IDENTIFYING MILITARY UNIFORMS

The chances are that you have a photograph or two of the soldier you are researching in uniform. As well as providing a direct link to the past, the insignia and badges can tell you something about his service.

Officers and other ranks wore differently designed uniforms. It is always clear which was which. Officers' uniforms were better tailored and officers were never seen without a tie. Ordinary soldiers wore coarser tunics and trousers (kilts of course in the Highland regiments). NCOs wore downward-pointing chevrons (one for a lance corporal, two for a corporal and three for a sergeant) on each arm above the elbow. They can be confused with long-service stripes which were worn below the elbow on the left sleeve.

Each regiment and corps had its own badge which was worn on the cap or as buttons on the jacket and tunic. A few are very distinctive, such as the mounted gun for the Royal Artillery (RA), but sometimes it can be difficult to work out exactly what the regiment was.

A contemporary drawing showing an officer's uniform and some of the badges you might find on it. (Author's collection)

There is quite an art to understanding what all the badges and symbols mean, but fortunately there are various guides to help you. The best books are Neil Storey, *Military Photographs and How to Date Them*, Countryside Books, 2009, and Robert Pols, *Identifying Old Army Photographs*, Family History Partnership, 2011. For regimental badges see Ian Swinnerton, *Identifying Your World War I Soldier from Badges and Photographs*, Family History Partnership, 2004, and Peter Doyle and Chris Foster, *British Army Cap Badges of the First World War*, Shire, 2010, which are excellent introductions.

Online there are several guides, although for once the Long, Long Trail is not the place to start. Probably the best general introduction to interpreting uniforms is provided at www.4thgordons.com/I-Spybook%20of%20Uniforms1.2.pdf. There are several sites that can help identify regimental badges, but the best is probably Roger Capewell's at www.militarybadges.org.uk/badget11.htm.

Further Reading

Records
There are several books that can provide additional information about the records:

William Spencer, *First World War Army Service Records*, TNA, 2008 provides a detailed if slightly dated guide to these records.

William Spencer, *Medals: The Research Guide,* TNA, 2006.

Neil Storey, *Military Photographs and How to Date Them*, Countryside Books, 2009.

Howard Williamson, *The Great War Collectors Companion,* Anne Williamson, 2011 contains a very valuable chapter on the medal index cards and how to interpret them.

The Medals Yearbook, Token Publishing, annually.

Background
Peter Duckers, *British Campaign Medals of the First World War*, Shire, 2011.

Richard Holmes, *Tommy: The British Soldier on the Western Front,* Harper, 2005.

John Lewis-Stempel, *Six Weeks: The Short and Gallant Life of the British Officer in the First World War: The Life and Death of the British Officer in the First World War*, Orion, 2011.

Richard van Emden, *The Soldier's War: The Great War Through Veterans' Eyes*, Bloomsbury, 2009.

The Long, Long Trail (www.1914-1918.net) has much background information which can help you interpret and understand the records.

Chapter 4

RESEARCHING SOLDIERS – ADDITIONAL RESOURCES

You don't have to stick to service records or, where appropriate, casualty records when researching your Army ancestors. There are lots of additional resources that may well shed light on a man's military career.

War Diaries

After the service records and medal index cards, war diaries are the most important source in both researching individuals and the histories of particular army units because they are a daily record of the unit's activities. They are official records and have no connection with private diaries kept by individuals. War diaries were introduced in 1908 and are still kept by units in wartime today.

As the name suggests, the diaries were designed to record unit activities, particularly when it was in action. This, it was felt, would help analysis by historians and strategists so that they could learn lessons for future wars, so they can be seen as being the first draft of history. They were kept by infantry battalions and artillery batteries as well as by higher echelons, such as brigades, divisions and even armies, as well as by more specialist units such as mobile hospitals, signals companies and field bakeries.

War diaries were often written up by the unit adjutant, who was otherwise responsible for the general administration of the unit, and signed off by the commanding officer each month. The ones that are the most interesting and important are battalion war diaries for the infantry as these record the fighting in some detail.

Inevitably, they reflect the enthusiasm that the officer compiling the war diary had for the task, but most are reasonably detailed, particularly when the unit was in the front line. Most were completed in the heat of battle or shortly afterwards.

Originally, they also contained regimental orders, plans of attack, maps and other ephemeral information, including occasional lists of officers and men awarded gallantry medals. Unfortunately, at some stage the diaries

```
                                    -8-
NOMINAL ROLL OF KILLED,WOUNDED & MISSING - Contd.            "D" Coy.

Regtl.No.    Rank and Name        Coy.  Nature of Casualty       Date

8/16540     A/C.S.M. Mangan.P.     D         Gassed           27.4.16
8/15678     Sergt. Keane. D.       D         Killed           27.4.16
8/16539     Sergt. Moyler.G.       D         Killed           27.4.16
8/15644     Sergt. Ryan.P.         D         Missing          27.4.16
8/16215     Sergt. Dunne.P.        D         Killed           27.4.16
8/16517     L/Sergt. Byrd.B.       D         Gassed           27.4.16
8/16492     L/Sergt. Croome.G.     D         Killed           27.4.16
8/21150     Corpl. Lennox.M.       D         Killed           27.4.16
8/16286     Corpl. Shea.W.         D         Killed           27.4.16
8/15655     Corpl. Fahey.J.        D         Killed           27.4.16
8/19312     L/Corpl. Cronin.T.     D         Killed           27.4.16
8/19683     L/Corpl. Dinneen.F.    D         Missing          27.4.16
8/15654     L/Corpl. Douglas.W.    D         Killed           27.4.16
8/22859     L/Corpl. Duffy.P.F.    D         Missing          27.4.16
8/19943     L/Corpl. McDonnell.J.            Wounded          27.4.16
8/16261     L/Corpl. Mullen.P.     D         Killed           27.4.16
8/19797     L/Corpl. Rice.J.       D         Missing          27.4.16
8/19974     L/Corpl. O'Rourke.M.             Gassed           27.4.16
8/19763     L/Corpl. Wheeler.P.    D         Wounded          27.4.16
8, 5363     L/Corpl. Harris.W.     D         Wounded          27.4.16
8/22858     L/Corpl. Byrne.G.      D         Wounded          27.4.16
25040       L/Corpl. Ryan.M.       D         Gassed           27.4.16

8/19371     Pte. Barbour.W.        D         Gassed           29.4.16
8/21849     Pte. Burke.J.          D         Gassed           27.4.
8/19133     Pte. Butler.J.         D         Killed
```

Unusually in the war diary of the 8th battalion Royal Dublin Fusiliers, April 1916 there is a list of men who were injured or killed during the gas attack of 27 April. (TNA WO 95/1974)

were weeded and some of this material was destroyed, although many maps are now in series WO 153. They can be very informative with plans for raids on enemy lines or in the case of the 8th Devonshire Regiment, detailed plans for the battalion's attack on German trenches on the 'first day on the Somme', 1 July 1916 (TNA WO 95/1655).

There may also be typewritten operational reports, which supplement entries in the war diaries themselves. The 8th Devonshire's war diary contains a detailed account for its attack on a German-held road near Martinpuich on the Somme during the morning of 20 July 1916. Of the 20 officers and 543 other ranks involved, 8 officers and 193 other ranks were either killed or wounded (that is just over a third). The report laconically notes: 'The operation was greatly hindered by the barrages falling short and in so doing causing casualties in our ranks and allowing the enemy to man his trenches and keep up a heavy fire.' It was during this attack that Private Theodore Veale won his Victoria Cross for rescuing an officer.

An almost complete set of diaries is at TNA is in series WO 95 (with a few 'confidential war diaries' in WO 154, which generally mention individuals who appeared before courts martial). They are arranged by army, corps, division and brigade, although in practice this doesn't matter because the online Catalogue contains a reference to each war diary. The diaries are arranged by month and consist of entries in pencil on loose sheets of paper.

Fortunately, TNA is digitising the diaries for units that mainly served in France and Flanders with the intention of placing them online by August 2014. A small selection is already available through the Online Records Service at £3.36 per piece, which usually contains diaries from two or three separate battalions or other units, so this represents excellent value. The chances are that these individual diaries will be unavailable for short periods in the reading rooms while they are being filmed for the project. Otherwise you need to visit Kew to consult the originals, many of which are now very frail and can be hard to read as they were generally written in pencil on thin greyish paper.

Their Value

Even if your ancestor is not mentioned in them, war diaries are the major source for discovering what his unit did day by day, covering his time in billets behind the line or on training exercises as well as tours of duty on the front line, relieving other units in quiet sectors or taking part in set-piece actions.

If he was killed or was wounded in action, you can usually find out roughly the circumstances. For Private William Maben, 5th King's Shropshire Light Infantry, it was on a big attack on German lines near Glencorse Wood/Hooge Crater, which lay about 3 miles south-east of Ypres, during the Battle of Passchendaele. He was one of 12 men who were reported as being missing during the day (which is why he appears on the memorial to the missing at Tyne Cot cemetery), in addition an officer and 19 other ranks were killed in action and 4 officers and 107 soldiers were wounded, many seriously. The war diary for 22 August 1917 (TNA WO 95/1902) was written up by the battalion commander, Lieutenant Colonel H M Smith, in some detail. In it he wrote that 'considerable opposition was encountered during the advance, especially by machine gun fire . . . a fourth of my battalion had by this time become casualties'. A picture of the area in 1919, showing a totally decimated landscape, is at www.ww1battle-fields.co.uk/flanders/hooge.html.

Just over a year earlier Lieutenant Eric Roper MC was probably seriously wounded as the result of a prolonged German bombardment on the company headquarters, where as adjutant he would have been based. The war diary (TNA WO 95/1350) for the 17th Royal Fusiliers for 11 September 1916 says: 'Enemy bombarded support lines and battn HQrs for several hours in the afternoon. Also our front line with trench mortars Battn HQr damaged Lt E Roper and 6OR [other ranks] wounded.'

It is also sometimes possible to find how a gallantry medal was awarded, particularly an immediate award, which is one that is given in the field for a specific act of bravery. As adjutant, Lieutenant Eric Roper was in an unusual position when he had to write up the award of his own Military Cross. On 8 July 1916 he recorded:

At 1.15am a party of 70 men under command of Capt Stewart, Lt Pollock and Lt Wootton attempted raid on hostile trenches opposite centre Picquet, left Cox. A few men succeeded in entering the German trenches. Pte White W N captured machine gun, but was hit on his way back and had to leave it behind. Capt Stewart reached German trench but was seriously wounded. He was brought in by Cpl Boehr who was awarded DCM. Capt Stewart and Lt Wootton were awarded Military Cross, Lt Wootton was also wounded (shock), Lt Pollock missing. 7 OR missing and 13 wounded. Other decorations awarded were Pte White DCM, Ptes Wiltshire, Trimbey and Sharcool Military Medals, Lt Roper Military Cross.

The citation to Roper's MC stated that it was awarded for rescuing a man who had been caught on the wire in no-man's-land.

Pitfalls

Some war diaries are missing, either because they were destroyed in enemy action (as was the case with the 1st Norfolk's diary for August and September 1914) or have subsequently been destroyed. In addition, war diaries were normally only completed by units on active service, which mean in a theatre of operations outside the British Isles.

However, a small number of diaries, which generally refer to courts martial of individual soldiers, were transferred to series WO 154 many years ago, so it is worth checking here as well.

It is unusual to find other ranks mentioned, unless they were the recipient of an immediate gallantry award, and even then they might not. There's no mention in the 8th Devonshire's war diary, for example, of the award of the Victoria Cross to Private Veale or the award of the Distinguished Conduct Medal, an award second only to the Victoria Cross, to Lance Corporal James Byars. However, officers are almost always mentioned, particularly when they are killed or wounded or less often when have been awarded medals or returned from leave or a training course.

The quality of the entries inevitably varies depending on who is writing the diary and the events they cover. There is no mention, for example, of any casualties in the war diary of the 18th King's Royal Rifle Corps for 26 October 1918, so it is impossible to work out except in very general terms how my Great-Uncle Stanley Crozier was killed.

Another pitfall is knowing exactly where a battalion or unit was based. The 8th Dubliners, for example, spent much of the winter of 1916/17 in York House trenches and in rest camps around Locre, including the evocatively named Butterfly Farm. It is not always easy to work out where these trenches were located, so you may need to obtain the appropriate trench maps (see Chapter 3) or ask fellow members in the appropriate online forums.

Lastly, it is important to remember that the unit or battalion and its constituent parts, such as companies or platoons, may have been located some distance from the unit headquarters and as a result may have had markedly different experiences to that recorded in the war diary.

Alternatives

If the war diary you want is missing, it is worth contacting the regimental archives to see whether they can help, because two copies were made and duplicates normally ended up with the regiment. Several regimental archives have transcribed war diaries in their possession and have put them online. These include:

- Berkshire and Wiltshire unit war diaries at www.thewardrobe.org.uk.

- East Surrey and King's Royal West Surrey unit war diaries at http://qrrarchive.websds.net/menu2.aspx?reg=WSR.

The brigade or division war diaries can provide some detail if the battalion war diary is missing and in any case are worth looking at if you are researching a particular battle or action.

Entries in war diaries can sometimes be supplemented by personal diaries and memoirs, and unofficial and official histories.

Gallantry Medals

Gallantry medals were awarded for acts of heroism and bravery on the field of battle. Some medals were awarded immediately for special acts (sometimes referred to as being awarded 'in the field'), while others – known as non-immediate – might be awarded weeks or months after the act.

The best known gallantry medal is the Victoria Cross. Biographies of the 633 men who won the award during the First World War, together with descriptions of their exploits, are described in an excellent series of books by Gerald Gliddon. There are also several websites devoted to VC winners, although Wikipedia, which has detailed biographies of each man, is probably the best place to start. A register of VC winners can be found in series WO 98 at TNA, together with copies of their citations, and other information is also available online the Online Records Service.

The Distinguished Service Order (DSO) was normally only awarded to senior officers, while the Military Cross (MC) was awarded for acts of bravery to officers of the rank of captain or below. The equivalents for NCOs and other ranks were the Distinguished Conduct Medal (DCM) and Military Medal (MM).

In many cases, non-immediate gallantry awards were given out almost randomly to members of a platoon or company who had seen action. Often men were asked to nominate comrades who should be honoured.

If there isn't a family story about the award of a gallantry medal, or the medal itself, you should find a note on the medal index card or, more rarely, in the service record.

An example of the Military Medal. (Author's collection)

Details of all gallantry awards were published in the *London Gazette*, sometimes with a citation, that is a short description of why the medal was awarded. For Major Eric Roper the citation for his Military Cross (MC), which appeared in the *London Gazette* on 18 August 1916, reads: 'For conspicuous gallantry when rescuing wounded men and directing stretcher-bearers. He personally carried a badly wounded man from the enemy's wire, though fired at and bombed. He was instrumental in saving many lives.' At the very least you will get the man's name, service number (not officers), rank, regiment and the date when the award was made. For awards of the Military Medal (MM) this is the only information you are likely to find. If your man was in the RA, Findmypast has a list of men who won the Military Medal with the date their award was gazetted.

Citations for awards of the Distinguished Conduct Medal (DCM) can be found on both Ancestry and Findmypast. They often, but not always, duplicate what is in the *London Gazette* but are certainly easier to find.

The awards of gallantry medals to both officers and, to an extent, other ranks are normally mentioned in war diaries. If you are lucky, you may be able to work out exactly for what reason the medal was awarded. The battalion war diary of 8th Royal Dublin Fusiliers for 11 February 1917 records that '14870 Cpl Horton H, 22916 Cpl Jones W, "D" Company awarded the Military Medal for throwing a live aerial torpedo out of the trench over the parapet where it exploded immediately' (WO 95/1974).

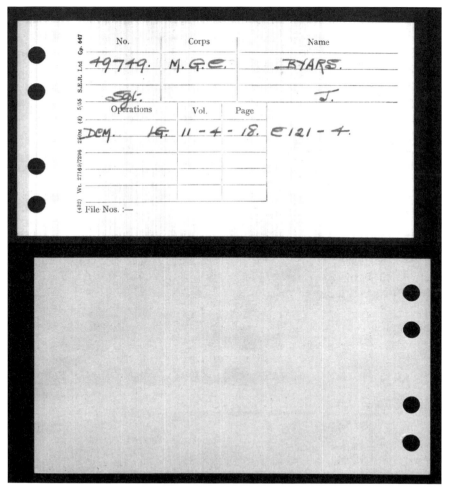

Card noting the award of the Distinguished Conduct Medal to Lance Corporal James Byars, Machine Gun Corps. (Ancestry/TNA WO 372)

TNA has a number of series of registers to gallantry awards. These, however, just contain copies of the relevant pages from the *London Gazette*, although the accompanying indexes may occasionally help identify which issue of the *Gazette* your man appears in, if the *Gazette's* website search engine fails to identify him.

There should also be cards in the medal index cards collection (see Chapter 3) for men who were awarded the DCM and MM. They give you little more than the date and page number in the *London Gazette* where the award is listed. In my experience, the reference is often wrong, but it can be useful if the *Gazette's* own website lets you down. For Sergeant James Byars, Machine Gun Corps, the card says his DCM was gazetted on 11 April 1918, but in fact it does not appear until 1 May.

The award of medals to individuals may also feature in newspaper stories. VC winners in particular were lauded by local dignitaries and were likely to appear at many functions in support for the war. On occasion one can imagine the extreme embarrassment many of these men must have felt. The pages of the *Western Times* in September 1916 are full of tributes and receptions to the local labourer and roughneck Theodore Veale, who won the Victoria Cross during the Somme. A man, one feels, that the mayor and corporation of Dartmouth would otherwise have never noticed unless he had appeared before them on a charge of drunkenness or breaking and entry (as he did in 1912).

The most common award was the Mention in Despatches (MiD) for acts of bravery or service that warranted reward, but was not enough to merit a gallantry award. During the war just over 2 per cent of the men in the British forces (141,082 officers and other ranks) were so honoured. At the time the only reward was to appear in the *London Gazette*, but subsequently King George V authorised the issue of a commemorative letter to holders and men were entitled to wear a stylised bronze oak leaf on their medal ribbons. The fact that a man was awarded a MiD is usually shown on the medal index card (often abbreviated to EM or EMB with a date when the award was published in the *Gazette*). There may also be separate cards for each MiD awarded with the approximate date the award was gazetted in the Medal Index Cards. These cards also include entries for the Meritorious Service Medal (MSM), which was given to NCOs for non-war-related service.

Further Reading

More about medals (both gallantry and campaign) can be found in William Spencer's *Medals: The Research Guide*, TNA, 2006 and Peter Duckers, *British Military Medals: a Guide for Collectors and Researchers*, Pen & Sword, 2009. Also useful is the *Medals Yearbook* produced by Token Publishing annually and another series of short books by Peter Duckers for Shire Books. There are various specialist books for many of the medals, often listing recipients and perhaps describing how the medals were won, such as R W Walker and Chris Buckland, *Citations of the Distinguished Conduct Medal, 1914–1920*, Naval & Military Press, 2007. TNA and regimental museums have copies of many of these books.

GOOD CONDUCT AND LONG SERVICE AWARD MEDALS

In 1833 a Long Service and Good Conduct Medal was instituted for soldiers who had served eighteen years in the Army, without a major blemish to their character. Medal rolls are in WO 102 at TNA. Men so rewarded also received extra pay. Incidentally, good conduct badges were awarded to soldiers after two, five, twelve and eighteen years' service. The badges took the form of chevrons, worn on the left cuff with the point of chevron uppermost (that is towards the elbow), with one chevron for each period completed. To the unwary they look like corporals or sergeants stripes, but they are worn further down the uniform jacket or tunic.

In 1846 a Meritorious Service Medal was authorised for sergeants and warrant officers who had performed good service other than in battle. From 1916 they could also awarded for gallantry or meritorious service when not in the face of the enemy. These awards are announced in *London Gazette* and you should also find a card in the medal index cards (see Chapter 3). Recipients were also allowed to use the letters MSM after their name. Registers for meritorious service are in WO 101 at TNA.

Courts Martial

A note on Private Gilbert Bailey, RAMC's service record about his court martial. (Ancestry/TNA WO 363)

A page from the Field Court Martial Register for 1917. (TNA WO 213/12)

Nearly 300,000 soldiers and 6,000 officers faced courts martial during the war, generally for being absent without leave, petty theft or drunkenness. The Casualty Form in the service record will record misdemeanours and should indicate whether your ancestor was put on a charge. 96516 Private Gilbert Bailey, RAMC, for example, on 19 March 1918 'received 3 days CB (confined to barracks) for being in a café during prohibited hours'. In general he was a man who perhaps lived life to the full as later in that year he was admitted to hospital with a case of gonorrhoea, presumably caught from a local prostitute.

Registers of courts martial in WO 90 (for men serving overseas) and WO 92 (for men on home duty) at TNA give brief details of the offence. Details of more serious offences can be found in registers in WO 213 and files in WO 71 and WO 93. See also TNA's Online Research Guide *Courts martial and desertion in the British Army 17th–20th centuries*.

The story of the 306 men 'shot at dawn', generally for trifling offences, is told in Julian Putkowski and Julian Sykes, *Shot at Dawn*, Pen & Sword, 1998. There is a series of files relating to their courts martial in series WO 71. Almost all of them were pardoned in 2005 by the British Government and notes to this effect were added to their files.

Prisoners of War

Nearly 200,000 British and Commonwealth prisoners of war fell into the hands of the Germans and their allies during the war, about half of whom were captured during the last six months of the war. Conditions could be grim, in part because of deliberate mistreatment, but more often because of increasing problems within Germany itself. Many prisoners eventually depended largely on food from Red Cross parcels, which were collected and packed by voluntary organisations under the leadership of the British Red Cross.

Unfortunately, it is difficult to find out very much about individual POWs, largely because detailed Red Cross registers and other records were lost in the late 1920s. A list of prisoners in German and Turkish hands in 1916 can be found in piece AIR 1/892/204/5/696-698 at TNA which indicates where a prisoner was captured and when, where they are held and their next of kin. However, the vast majority of prisoners were captured during the much more fluid warfare which occurred after March 1918, particularly during the German advances in the spring which saw many British positions overwhelmed.

There is a published *List of Officers taken Prisoner in the Various Theatres of War between August 1914 and November 1918*, 1919, repr. 1988, which is online at Findmypast and copies are in TNA and SOG libraries. Entries vary but in general they are not terribly informative. For 2/Lieutenant Ivan

A group of British prisoners of war. (Author's collection)

One of the few surviving letters from my Great-Uncle Stanley Crozier, a scribbled note about badges required for his uniform. (Adrian Lead)

Campbell, for example, it is just recorded that he was captured on 17 September 1918 and repatriated on 8 December.

Returning British prisoners were interrogated by the authorities about their experiences and a selection of these reports (with an index) can be downloaded from TNA's Online Records Service. They were intended to be used as evidence of German brutality in war crimes trials which were planned after the war, but in the event did not take place. While the reports are rather biased therefore, they make interesting reading.

The service records of officers who became prisoners should include a statement indicating how the man was captured. This was presented to the court martial set up to investigate the circumstances. In almost all cases the officer was exonerated. 2/Lieutenant Ivan Campbell, 11th Cameron

Highlanders, was captured taking the rum ration up to his men on 17 September 1918. He got lost and then his batman (servant) was shot by a sniper: 'By this time it was six o'clock and very light and as I had not located the post I was determined to wait until dark and get back to head-quarters. Just after dark as I preparing to get away I was seized by a German patrol . . .' (TNA WO 339/123743). Perhaps nervous of what the court martial might think, Campbell added at the end of his statement: 'As the patrol consisted of nine men I was forcibly prevented from using my revolver.' Campbell was taken back to the German company headquarters and sent back up the line to Lille and then to the camp at Rastatt in Germany.

There are occasional mentions of individual prisoners and their condi-tions in the correspondence of the Foreign Office Prisoner of War Department (FO 383) at Kew, although the department was largely respon-sible for civilian internees. This correspondence has been summarised and is available through TNA's Catalogue.

Some records can also be found at the IWM. The Women's War Work Collection, for example, contains many postcards from prisoners acknowl-edging the receipt of Red Cross parcels as well as correspondence from the various charities involved in the provision of these parcels.

The International Committee of the Red Cross (ICRC) in Geneva was responsible for passing details of prisoners of war between the various combatant nations and ensuring that conditions in the camps were adequate. Voluminous records were maintained but these are closed for 100 years, although the archivists will search the records for you. You need to contact the ICRC Archives, 19 avenue de la Paix, CH-1202 Genève, Switzerland. More information can be found at www.icrc.org. The records are now being properly sorted and should be available online by 2014.

Perhaps the most extraordinary of all collections from the First World War is at the National Sound Archive, which has sixty-six recordings made of British and Irish prisoners of war during the First World War by German academics from the Lautarchive at Berlin's Humboldt University. The pris-oners read out the 'Parable of the Prodigal Son' from the New Testament so their accents could be studied. About half the men are named, the rest are anonymous. You can listen to the recordings at http://sounds.bl.uk.

Further Reading

The records and experiences of the men are described in more detail in Sarah Paterson, *Tracing Your Prisoner of War Ancestors, the First World War*, Pen & Sword, 2012.

More about the experience of POWs can found in Richard van Emden, *Prisoners of the Kaiser: the last POWs of the Great War*, Pen & Sword, 2000 and Robert Jackson, *The Prisoners 1914–1918*, Routledge, 1989.

REGIMENTAL MAGAZINES

One of the most prized sources held by regimental archives is the regimental magazine. These magazines are likely to be of most interest if you are researching men who were either pre-war regulars or made a career in the Army after the Armistice as relatively few seem to have been published during the war itself.

By the 1920s almost every regiment published a quarterly magazine which contained many stories about regimental activities and listing promotions, the awards of education certificates, cups for marksmanship and the minutiae of everyday life in the Army which on the whole was not recorded elsewhere.

One of the earliest was the *Suffolk Regimental Gazette*, which was first published between February 1890 and July 1959, except for the periods between October 1914 and December 1915 and January 1917 to June 1920. Regular features included photographs, births, marriages and deaths; detailed lists of appointments, promotions, awards of certificates; sporting and social events; and articles about the regiment's history and traditions.

There is no national collection of these magazines, although the NAM and to a lesser degree the IWM have incomplete sets. The best place to look is in regimental archives. The Royal Logistics Corps has published online those for its 'forming corps', notably the Army Service Corps and Army Ordnance Corps. Details are available at www.rlcarchive.org. Miles Templer (www.templer.net) has published a small selection on CD.

Pensions

One of most disappointing gaps in the records concerns pension records because very few survive.

Widows and disabled ex-servicemen were entitled to claim a pension. Much ill-feeling was created by the low level of the pension and the difficulties placed in the way of claimants by the government and local officials supervising the grant of awards.

Detailed records were naturally kept, but most have long since been destroyed. However, series PIN 82 at TNA contains an 8 per cent sample of widows' and dependents' papers arranged in alphabetical order. This includes sailors and airmen as well as soldiers. The forms give personal details of each serviceman's name, place of residence, particulars of service and the date, place and cause of death or injury. They also give details of the assessment of, and entitlement to, pension awards, the amount awarded and the length of time for which the award is granted. Often there are plaintive letters from old soldiers or their families asking for increases in their pensions, usually with little success.

Another sample of pensions awarded in the London area is in PIN 26 and some claims for pensions awarded before the First World War are in PIN 71. And just possibly, it may also be worth looking at the registered files of the Ministry of Pensions in PIN 15.

There are several series of records relating to wartime claims made by officers and their families in series PMG 42-PMG 47, but the information here largely notes the address of the individual (or the recipient of the pension) and the amount paid each month or quarter.

More complete is a set of post-First World War pension appeal records at the National Records of Scotland (www.nrscotland.gov.uk) in series PT6. The records contain detailed pension applications from thousands of Scottish soldiers and their next of kin (usually widows). They are the Scottish equivalent of PIN 26 series for England and Wales, but appear to be complete.

PENSION RECORD CARDS

As this book was going to press the WFA announced that it had acquired several million soldiers' pension record cards from the MoD. There are cards for officers, other ranks who either died or were wounded during the war and received a pension, together with their widows and dependants. They are important because, uniquely, they unite genealogical information with military information, so, for example, it is now possible easily to find an individual's unit. As important, the records provide information on those who came back, and who were entitled to a pension, for which there is often scant detail elsewhere.

The WFA is scanning the cards and will make them available online in due course. Until then unfortunately they are not accessible to the public.

Personal Papers and Effects

Soldiers (and indeed for that matter sailors and airmen) wrote about their experiences at the time in letters and diaries and perhaps in old age they wrote their memoirs. That they did this is not surprising: they were witnessing events unique in human history. An increasing number are appearing in print or on websites.

There was a very efficient postal service which meant that letters and parcels generally only took a few days to go from Britain to the Western Front (although deliveries elsewhere could be more erratic). Most soldiers took advantage of this and scribbled regular letters home. Because of censorship and the wish not to frighten their families, these letters tend to be fairly anodyne reassuring the reader that they were well, perhaps indicating that they were safe behind the lines and asking for items to be sent out. The only surviving letter from my Great-Uncle Stanley Crozier asks my grandmother to buy a variety of badges for his uniform. In general, they are not great works of literature, but even so after nearly a century they are treasured family heirlooms.

Officers' letters tend to be better written and more informative – after all they were trusted not to give the game away. On 31 March 1917, for example, Captain Frederick Chapman, Royal Fusiliers, wrote to his mother:

> I was most delighted to get two letters from you the day before yesterday and your jolly parcel today. We all enjoyed the rock cakes at tea today and the oranges are in excellent condition. Very many thanks for the razor blades (which will last me a long time) and the soap Wright's Coal Tar is the kind I like best. The watch has not come but will be in the next parcel . . .
>
> I am immensely fit. I ride practically every day. I was in the saddle from 10–1 today. I simply love it – galloping especially . . .
>
> Tomorrow is Sunday and on Monday we start marching. We shall probably be marching for a week. There is no doubt that we are going to a new part of the line and I am glad . . .
>
> I have been so happy out here and like the soldier's life so well (except in parts) that I have thought about getting a regular commission . . . (Imperial War Museum: Chapman Collection)

Unfortunately, Captain Chapman lost an eye two months later which put paid to any hope of a permanent Army career.

Neither officers nor men were allowed to keep diaries, although clearly many did. Some were just simple entries about the weather and where the unit was located in a pocket diary. Others were much more elaborate affairs. In a post-war preface to his diary Private Sydney Fuller, 8th Suffolks, wrote of how he kept his diary, which covered almost the whole period of the war:

> This diary was never carried into actual 'action', but was always left with a comrade who was not going 'into the lines' with full instructions as to what should be done in the event (sometimes very probable, always possible) of the owner's 'going west'.
>
> The other great difficulty was getting the diary 'home'. In this case, it was smuggled home in small batches, sometimes in a 'green envelope' (an abuse of a privilege which abuse meant at least a court-martial if detected) and sometimes being taken to England by comrade, proceeding on leave, concealed in the layers of the said comrade's puttees, or in other odd places. . . .

Parts of the diary are a little 'sketchy' but the reason for this is easily understood. No diary was written when actually 'in the line' so that sometimes the events when recorded were nearly a fortnight old. At the rate things happened sometimes, there were quite a number of happenings to record by that time, and many interesting details were often forgotten or imperfectly remembered . . . what has been written, however, is strictly true. . . . (IWM, Fuller Collection)

Memoirs are also important. Some are based on diaries and letters or correspondence with old comrades, while others were clearly written decades later for the grandchildren or to exercise old ghosts. But they can be very revealing. Private Stanley Bradbury, 1/5th Seaforth Highlanders, wrote a typescript memoir 'The War According to S Bradbury' in 1923, which is now at the IWM. It is based on a diary he kept at the time. At the end of March 1917 his unit was based at Acq in Northern France but they were starving because the rations for the platoon had not arrived:

However, I knew that on the Saturday, all being well, I should receive the weekly 3s which I had arranged with Mother to send me, out of my money, and my pal (Middy) and I eagerly looked forward to this coming so that we could have at least one feed during the week. The effect of having so little to eat for a week was plainly telling on us. On the Saturday afternoon our luck appeared to be in as there was the good news from home that the letter had arrived, and I sought out my pal to tell him the good news that the letter had arrived, so together we opened it and found to our bitter disappointment that there was no postal order in the explanation being that as we were moving it was likely to get lost. It was impossible to find words to express our intense disappointment and we both slunk away in silence and misery. . . . (IWM: Bradbury Collection)

Or you might just have an ancestor's medals, Army service discharge paper, pay book or photographs. For my Great-Uncle Stanley my cousin has his medals (proudly framed in the dining room), a letter and his will, a photograph, letters from his commanding officer and the battalion padre written to his mother after his death attesting to his good work as a soldier, and several appeals from the Rifle Corps to help build a battalion war memorial. They are of course much treasured.

Personal papers can be found in a variety of places, although of course the most likely location remains people's attics and shoeboxes. Sometimes you might be lucky in finding something very special. I remember being very jealous when I was shown immaculately preserved scrapbooks of three brothers' Army service with photographs, postcards and letters, including some from a prisoner of war camp where one of the brothers spent a few months in 1918.

If you have such a collection it is well worth considering donating it to the IWM or a local record office or regimental archive. They may be willing to give you a set of copies in return for the originals. Certainly you should think about making some provision for their care in your will.

There is no central list of what personal papers are to be found where, although it is worth checking the NRA to see whether a collection of papers has been identified by them (www.nationalarchives.gov.uk/nra).

The IWM has the most important collection of personal papers. Many are described in the Museum's catalogue at www.iwm.org.uk/collections/search.

Another important resource is the Liddle Collection at Leeds University's Brotherton Library with over 4,000 collections of private papers. Details can be accessed at http://library.leeds.ac.uk/liddle-collection.

Regimental archives and the NAM are also good sources (and for the RN and RAF the RNM and RAFM respectively). The Royal Artillery Archives in Woolwich, for example, has much for the First World War, particularly for officers. Very few of these archives have catalogues on their websites, so you will have to contact them to see whether they can help. In addition, small collections can sometimes be found at local record offices, and these might include material for civilian war workers.

Lastly, an increasing number of diaries and memoirs in particular are being published or appearing online, so try Google and Amazon for books (www.amazon.co.uk). There are several excellent websites that have republished letters and memoirs, including Edward Deane, Hampshire Regiment (http://e-d-deane-war-memoirs.blogspot.co.uk/), Arthur's Letters – Arthur Dease, a volunteer ambulanceman (www.arthursletters.com), Reg Knight in the Royal Engineers (www.petergknight.com/warletters.html) and Harry Lamin, York and Lancaster Regiment (wwar1.blogspot.co.uk/2006/07/private-harry-lamin.html).

The IWM and other museums have impressive collections of ephemera, which in the case of the IWM itself can be seen in its online catalogue. A fascinating Europe-wide initiative to collect personal items from each of the participating nations is being collated by Europeana at www.europeana1914-1918.eu/en.

Photographs and Film

Although TNA has a small number of photographs (particularly aerial shots in WO 316), the largest collection by far is at the IWM. At the heart of the museum's collections are 40,000 official photographs of all aspects of the war. As it took time for a satisfactory system to be set up, and overcome suspicion from the military authorities, the photographic record is more comprehensive from mid-1916 onwards than for the first half of the war. This collection is supplemented by material donated by individual servicemen. The description of a few photographs and photographic collections can be found in the IWM online catalogue at www.iwmcollections.org.uk.

Regimental museums and local studies libraries may also have collections of material. The Honourable Artillery Company archive, for example, has many photographs of soldiers who fell during the war, because the company's secretary of the day wrote to the families of the deceased asking for copies.

The IWM's Film and Video Archive also has by far the largest collection of films, which is described in Roger Smithers (ed.), *The Imperial War Museum Film Catalogue Volume 1: The First World War*, Flick Books, 1997.

The best known film of the period is *The Battle of the Somme*, which was eventually seen by two-thirds of the British population on its release in late 1916. It is now available on YouTube or on video and is worth watching as it offers a unique picture of the British Army on the Western Front. You will recognise scenes from it as clips all too often appear in news stories or programmes about the war.

There are also a number of regional film archives, which may also have film of the period. The largest of these is the North West Film and Video Archive in Manchester.

It is also worth checking newsreels, which were short news stories shown at local cinemas. Those for the First World War largely concentrate on the 'home front' because of technical difficulties of having cameras near the front coupled with the British Army's paranoia over security. Details of 180,000 stories filmed between 1910 and 1983 are at http://bufvc.ac.uk/newsonscreen/search. Two of the major newsreels producers British Pathe (www.britishpathe.com) and Movietone (www.movietone.com) have made their clips available online free of charge, and the period of the First World War is included. Both websites are extremely easy to use, and you can search by name as well as by place or topic.

YouTube (www.youtube.com) also has a number of First World War themed videos and clips, including The *Battle of the Somme* mentioned above, but otherwise coverage is actually rather disappointing.

Trench Maps

A bird looking down on the Western Front would have seen a maze of trenches criss-crossing the pockmarked landscape, carrying men and material to the front line where the two enemies faced each other. From mid-1915 British surveyors and mapmakers began to map the trenches – initially on the German side, but from mid-1917 the British ones too.

Originally mapped at a scale of 1:10,000, roughly 6in to the mile, red lines (for German trenches) and blue (British) are superimposed on a ghostly backdrop of the villages, woods and railways found on pre-war maps of Flanders and France, upon which these maps were based. Ammunition dumps, hospitals and other facilities reveal how far the countryside for miles behind the front line was appropriated by the military. And close to the front line the maps show the intricacies of the trench systems indicating individual command posts, machine guns, field batteries and so on, all plotted from air photographs.

Many maps are very detailed, although it has to be said that they can be difficult to interpret unless you are an experienced map user. They will be of most use to people with considerable knowledge of the Western Front and the battles that were fought there. Even so it still comes as a surprise to discover how close the German lines really were to Ypres – 40 minutes steady march would have taken you to their front line.

Collections of maps are held by both TNA (mainly series WO 297) and the IWM. Local regimental museums and other archives may also have smaller collections.

Many maps, but certainly not all, have been scanned by McMaster University in Canada and can be viewed at http://library.mcmaster.ca/maps/ww1/ndx5to40.htm.

You can buy facsimiles in several ways. Paper copies of selected maps have been published by G H Smith and Son (www.ghsmith.com) and these can be bought directly from TNA's bookshop and military museums or online from the company.

Otherwise sets are available on CD. The best such collection is undoubtedly *The National Archives British Trench Map Atlas* produced by Naval & Military Press (www.great-war-trench-maps.com/watm.htm) with hundreds of different maps in various editions. The WFA has published a small collection for the major battle zones.

Great War Digital (www.greatwardigital.com) is a company selling digitised trench maps which can be used in GPS systems. They are in 3-D and look very impressive.

Further Reading

An excellent introduction to these maps and how to use them is at www.1914-1918.net/trench_maps.htm. There is also an explanatory essay at www.great-war-trench-maps.com/watm.htm. The best book on the subject remains Peter Chasseaud, *Topography of Armageddon: a British trench map atlas of the Western Front, 1914–1918*, Mapbooks, 1991; TNA has a copy.

Chapter 5

THE WAR AT SEA

The First World War of course did not take place solely on land. Naval actions were fought on all of the Seven Seas, convoys brought much-needed food and supplies across the Atlantic and the blockade starved Germany of vital raw materials and eventually brought her to her knees in the autumn of 1918. However, it can be difficult to find out very much about what individual seamen – RN or merchant – did or the actions they saw.

Royal Navy

In 1914 the RN was the most powerful and largest navy in the world, more than twice the size of the German navy. However, this mattered little in what became an essentially land war. For most of the war the Navy was engaged in boring but essential work in protecting the sea lanes to the British Isles. The only major sea battle, that fought at Jutland, was in effect a draw, although it had the major result of restricting the German High Seas Fleet to port for the rest of the war.

The manpower of the RN expanded from 250,000 at the start to 450,000 at the end of the war (even so this was less than a quarter of the strength of the Army). And the Royal Marines (RM), which is part of the Navy, rose from 17,000 men in 1914 to number over 55,000 in 1918.

NAVY OR WAVY NAVY?
Individual ratings and officers could join various parts of the RN – the Navy (RN) itself, Royal Marines (RM) and various auxiliary forces, notably the Royal Naval Reserve (RNR), the Royal Naval Volunteer Reserve (RNVR) (sometimes referred to as the Wavy Navy because of the distinct stripes worn by officers on their uniforms) and the Royal Naval Division (RND). Each has their own set of records, and if you are not sure to which one your man belonged then you may have to search in a number of different places to find him.

Common Sources

There are a few resources that cover the Navy (and where appropriate the Merchant Navy) as well as the Army. These include:

- The *London Gazette* which records the promotions and, to a degree, postings of officers as well as the award of gallantry medals (see Chapter 3).

- Records for RN (and RM) officers and men after about 1923 are still with the MoD (although I have found the occasional record for ratings later than this). If your ancestor served in the Navy between the wars, you need to obtain the record from the Service Personnel and Veterans Agency and details of how to do this can be found at www.veterans-uk.info/service_records/royal_navy.html. If you already know the ships he served in, it is probably not worth the expense as the information you receive is not much more informative.

- The Debt of Honour Register (CWGC) records the death of naval personnel (see below and Chapter 2).

- The UK National Inventory of War Memorials (www.ukniwm .org.uk) includes 550 specific memorials dedicated to men of the RN.

- Details of ratings and their officers who died during the war can be found in rolls of honour in much the same way as their Army comrades. A photograph and brief notes about Lieutenant Richard Donaldson RNVR MC who was a student at the University of Glasgow, for example, can be found on the university's roll of honour.

MATERIAL AT THE FLEET AIR ARM MUSEUM

During the 1990s, the museum's Centre for Naval Aviation Records and Research acquired a large collection of records from the MoD about naval and marine personnel which was not required by TNA. The majority of records are for non-commissioned personnel who enlisted in the RN and RM before about 1925. Of particular interest are the engagement books for men who joined between 1905 and 1921. These include details of date and place of joining, physical description, information about any previous military service and parent's consent if the entrant was a boy.

Also available are the papers of most of the men who were enlisted for short-service 'hostilities only' during the First World War.

> The records are described in more detail at www.fleetairarm.com/
> en-GB/royal_navy_royal_marines_services_documents.aspx.

Service Records

Royal Navy

Brief details of officers can be found in published Navy Lists. From these you are likely to be able to get an idea of when they entered, the branch they were in, subsequent promotions and the ship they were serving on at the time the List was published.

A set can be found on the open shelves in the Open Reading Room at TNA. Websites like TheGenealogist and FamilyRelatives have digitised the odd copy. TNA also has a set of Confidential Navy Lists which contain more information, including where an officer was serving, in series ADM 177.

It is expected that these records will be online at some stage.

Service records for officers and the non-commissioned warrant officers who served during the war are in ADM 196 and online through TNA's Online Records Service. You should find details of the officers' family and his date of birth, promotions and ships served on, together with brief notes

A page from the service record of Commander Alfred Carpenter VC. (TNA ADM 196/125)

about a man's performance. Another useful series is the summaries of confidential reports (also in ADM 196) which contain candid comments on individuals' abilities written by senior officers. Captain Alfred Carpenter, RN, VC, for example, was praised for being 'zealous and capable . . . very good navigating officer', but perhaps he made an enemy at some stage for he was criticised in the 1920s for 'lack of charm of personality. Fond of advertising and probably a good leader, although the former might sometimes affect his judgement' (TNA ADM 196/142, 90).

Ratings were divided into specialisms, known as trades, reflecting the work they did on board ships. This information is indicated in the prefixes and suffixes to the service number. A list of the most common prefixes can be found in TNA's In-Depth Guide *Royal Navy: Ratings* and a full list in Bruno Pappalardo, *Tracing your Naval Ancestors*, Public Record Office, 2003.

If you have photographs, trades may be identifiable from badges worn on the right-hand sleeve of uniforms. Incidentally, it is easy to be confused by the stripes on sailors' arms. These are good conduct stripes, awarded for varying periods

Commander Carpenter and a friend photographed after the award of the Victoria Cross for his actions during the raid on the German submarine pens at Zeebrugge, 23 April 1918. (Author's collection)

of service during which the sailor's yearly conduct assessment did not fall below 'very good'. In addition, the RN recruited boys from the age of 14 (the joining age in the Army was 18) and had a network of training ships – the most famous of which was HMS *Ganges* – teaching likely lads seacraft.

Records of ratings are in ADM 188 and are available through TNA's Online Records Service. They will tell you which ships a man served with, medals won, promotions and remarks about conduct and an indication of how and when he left the Navy. Incidentally, the abbreviation DD means

An extract from the service record for Petty Officer Ernest Highams with the circumstances of his death. (TNA ADM 188/240)

that he was discharged dead and the word 'run' indicates that he deserted. Generally the forms are easy to read.

There are several series of records that include material about pensions awarded to naval personnel, although you are only likely to find out how much was paid each quarter, to whom and their address. Claims by officers for pensions for wounds are in PMG 23/206-207 and PMG 42/13-14. PMG 56/1-9 has details of allowances made to widows, dependants and children of specially entered mercantile crews, and crews of mercantile ships commissioned as HM ships or auxiliary craft, who were killed during naval warlike operations. And details of pensions awarded to officers and men of the mercantile marine killed or injured in Admiralty employment are in PIN 15/1733-1736, while claims to pensions from members of the RNR are in PIN 15/209-211.

Auxiliary Forces
From the mid-nineteenth century the Navy maintained several auxiliary forces, which has allowed the Navy to maintain a trained reserve of men who can be called upon in times of war. Many of these men came from merchant shipping so there may be other records about them (see below). There were two main branches: the RNR – recruited from merchant seamen – and the larger RNVR – who came from the ranks of amateur seamen and the wider general public.

The RNR was established in 1859 as a reserve force of officers and men from deep-sea merchant ships and fishing vessels. At the outbreak of the First World War it had a strength of around 30,000 men.

Officers are listed in the Navy Lists. Information given includes name, rank, date of commission and seniority, as well as the ships on which the officers served. Service records up to 1920 are in ADM 240 at TNA. They are arranged by rank and seniority and show details of merchant as well as naval service and are arranged in numerical order of commission. There are no separate indexes but some of the pieces can be used as indexes. Additional information can often be found in the service cards and files in ADM 340.

The FAAM also has record cards for a number of RNR officers. The museum also has nearly a hundred pay and appointing ledgers for officers of the RNR (as well as those in the RNVR) for the First World War which can offer useful information on pay movements (including tax bills and probate) to complement the officers' records at TNA. And they have original records for RNR ratings from 1908 until after the Second World War. Incidentally, records of RNR ratings between 1914 and 1919 are available in ADM 337 (and via TNA's Online Records Service) with additional records in BT 377.

The Royal Fleet Auxiliary (RFA) was established in 1905 to provide coaling ships for the Navy and now replenishes and resupplies RN vessels around the world. Until 1921 the officers of the RFA were nearly all RNR officers and ranked accordingly. Since then they have been ranked as other Merchant Navy officers. The FAAM holds the crew books for RFA and Mercantile Fleet Auxiliary for the First World War. These contain alphabetical indexes of ships, crew lists (entries and discharges), rates of pay, next of kin, etc. The RFA Historical Society maintains an excellent website devoted to the RFA's history at www.historicalrfa.org with a roll of honour and descriptions of ships which have served in the RFA.

The RNR was generally confined to officers and men of deep-sea merchantmen but in 1911 it was felt that there was a need to employ trawlers in wartime as minesweepers and patrol vessels. The Royal Naval Reserve Trawler Section (RNR(T)) was set up to enrol the necessary personnel. Although abolished as a separate section of the RNR in 1921, the RNR(T) always remained quite distinct from the RNR proper. Service records of ratings who served in the RNR(T) are in BT 377. Their service numbers were prefixed with the letters DA, ES, SA, SB or TS. The records of ratings whose service numbers begin with SBC have not survived.

During the First World War there was a Mercantile Marine Reserve made up of merchant seamen serving on merchant vessels requisitioned by the Admiralty for wartime service. Some of these men may have been members of the RNR with records in BT 377 and they would have been eligible for the Mercantile Marine Medal for which there is a medal roll in BT 351 (and available via TNA's Online Records Service).

The RNVR, founded in 1903, was a force of officers and ratings who undertook naval training in their spare time, but were not professional seamen. Officers are listed in the Navy Lists. Service records of RNVR officers can be found in two series: ADM 337 and occasionally ADM 340. Records in ADM 337/117-128 cover the period up to 1922 and can be downloaded through TNA's Online Records Service. These pieces are also searchable by name here. Service records for ratings also in ADM 337 record when a man joined, which ships he served on and his fate. There is also a physical description. Z/3302 Thomas Fowler had been a porter when he joined up in September 1915. He joined HMS *Indefatigable* on 11 January 1916 and died in action on 31 May 1916. *Indefatigable* sunk during the Battle of Jutland with the loss of all but three lives. Details of medals awarded for service in the First World War are on Ancestry.

The RND was set up by the First Sea Lord, Winston Churchill, in the early weeks of the war to use a surplus of some 20,000–30,000 men of the RNR who would not find jobs on any ship of war, initially to help the Army defend Antwerp. They later served at Gallipoli and then in Flanders. In 1916 the RND was transferred to the Army as 63rd (Royal Naval) Division. Despite the fact that the division was operating in conditions very different from the high seas, naval discipline was maintained. Time continued to be regulated by bells as if aboard ship. Men referred to leaving the front line

The service record for Able Seaman Thomas Fowler who was killed at the Battle of Jutland when his ship HMS Indefatigable *was sunk with only ten survivors. (TNA ADM 337/38)*

as 'going ashore'. There was also a long-running battle over the wearing of beards, which were prohibited in the Army, but allowed in the Navy. Indeed, the brigades themselves were named after naval heroes: Anson, Benbow (disbanded in 1916), Collingwood (disbanded in 1916), Drake, Hawke, Hood, Howe and Nelson.

Service records for officers in the RND are in ADM 339/3, with the equivalent for ratings in ADM 339/1, although records of ratings who died on active service are in ADM 339/2. They are online through TNA's Online Records Service.

The service records can be pretty informative particularly for officers and for men killed in action. In all cases you will be given details of next of kin, date of birth and address, religion and civilian occupation together with a physical description. Within the division the card records movements and postings and, where appropriate, a date of when they were killed. For Lieutenant Richard Donaldson, RNVR, MC there are six cards (TNA WO 339/3) which record his career from his interview to become an officer in July 1915 to the date of his death on 5 September 1918. He became an officer in Anson Battalion and saw service in the Middle East and later on the Western Front, there are reports of the wounds he received, where he was treated and periods of sick leave and general leave. He later commanded 100th and 188th Trench Mortar battalion. His award of the Military Cross was gazetted on 1 January 1918.

Similar records are available for Able Seaman Joseph Donaldson of Hawke Battalion who had been a South Shields miner before enlisting in January 1915. He suffered from enteric fever while in the Middle East, and later served on the Western Front and was reported missing in action on 4 February 1917. He is commemorated on the great memorial to the missing at Thiepval on the Somme.

For men who died in service, the information is largely summarised in the database to the division's casualties and this is available on both Ancestry and Findmypast.

War diaries for the brigades into which the division was divided are in WO 95 (many of which can also be downloaded via TNA's Online Records Service) and ADM 137.

Casualties

Officers and ratings with no known graves are commemorated on memorials at Chatham, Portsmouth and Plymouth. After the First World War an appropriate way had to be found of commemorating those members of the RN who had no known grave. It was agreed that the three major naval ports – Chatham, Plymouth and Portsmouth – should each have an identical memorial of unmistakable naval form, an obelisk, which would serve as a leading mark for shipping. The memorial at Chatham commemorates 8,517 sailors of the First World War, including Z/3302 Able Seaman Thomas Fowler. The ones at Portsmouth and Plymouth commemorate around 10,000 and 7,251 respectively (plus many more from the Second World War).

Details of some 45,000 RN and RM officers and ratings who died during the First World War are listed in the War Graves Roll in ADM 242. The roll gives full name, rank, service number, ship's name, date and place of birth, cause of death, where buried and next of kin. The records are on Findmypast. The roll was based on a card index (also in ADM 242) which also gives the place of burial, such as 'Buried [in] East Africa on a small knoll marked by blazed tree, R. bank Kaibiga River, 100 yards W. of Ndyimbwa-Ungwara'. For those who fell at Gallipoli there are often detailed descriptions rather than traditional locations for the grave. Further registers of killed and wounded are in ADM 104/145-149.

Both Ancestry and Findmypast have a database of the casualties of the RND which includes a detailed summary of their career in the division.

There is an online list of naval casualties at http://naval-history.net which can be searched by name or by ship. Entries are quite detailed. The

World War 1 - Casualty Lists of the Royal Navy and Dominion Navies
Researched & compiled by Don Kindell

by Name - E - EACHUS to EYRES

Edited by Gordon Smith, Naval-History.Net

SS Leinster, lost 10 October 1918 with Royal Navy men onboard
(Dave Martin, click to enlarge)

on to Facer-Fysh

Notes:
(1) Casualty information in order - Surname, First name, Initial(s), Rank and part of the Service other than RN (RNR, RNVR, RFR, RMLI etc), Service Number (ratings only, also if Dominion or Indian Navies), (on the books of another ship/shore establishment, O/P – on passage), Fate
(2) Click for abbreviations
(3) Click here for **Month-by-Month** lists in the Casualties Homepage where more information may be found

E

EACHUS, Walter, Able Seaman, RNVR, Mersey Z 657, Black Prince, 31 May 1916, Jutland, ship lost
EADE, Arthur, Private, RMLI, 3719 (Po), RMLI, Portsmouth Division, 9 October 1916, illness
EADE, Arthur, Sick Berth Attendant, M 4062, Leinster, steamship (Colleen, O/P), 10 October 1918, ship lost
EADE, Ernest, Stoker 1c, SS 115352 (Ch), Kale, 27 March 1918, ship lost
EADE, Harold, Able Seaman, 219145 (Ch), Liberty, 28 August 1914, Heligoland Bight, surface action
EADE, Henry, Stoker 1c, K 17737 (Po), Queen Mary, 31 May 1916, Jutland, ship lost

A page of naval casualties to be found on the Naval-History.Net website. (Naval-History.Net)

one for Ernest Highams, for example, reads: 'HIGHAMS, Ernest E, Petty Officer, 162971 (Dev), Pegasus, 20 September 1914, ship lost'. And the one for Thomas Fowler: 'FOWLER, Thomas, Able Seaman, RNVR, London Z 3302, Indefatigable, 31 May 1916, Jutland, ship lost'.

In addition, naval casualties are listed in: S D and D B Jarvis, *The Cross of Sacrifice: Officers who Died in the Service of the RN, RNVR, RM, RNAS and RAF, 1914–1919*, Naval & Military Press, 2000 and S D and D B Jarvis, *The Cross of Sacrifice: Non-Commissioned Officers, Men and Women of the UK, Commonwealth and Empire Who Died in the Service of the Royal Naval Air Service, Royal Navy, Royal Marines, Royal Flying Corps and Royal Air Force 1914–1921*, Naval & Military Press, 1996. The libraries of TNA, RNM and SOG have copies.

Often captains' and other reports into actions involving naval ships will include lists of casualties. Generally, they just list the deceased's name, rank, trade and next of kin, but the reports themselves may indicate how he lost his life. The vast majority of these reports are in ADM 137, ADM 116 and ADM 1. There is no central list, but a search by name of the ship in each of these series in turn (perhaps starting with ADM 137) through TNA's Catalogue should turn up something. A list of the casualties for

The entry for Thomas Fowler in the list of the casualties for HMS Indefatigable *compiled by the Admiralty after the loss of the ship. (TNA ADM 116/1533)*

HMS *Indefatigable*, for example, is at ADM 116/1533. The entry for Thomas Fowler gives the name and address of the next of kin, in this case his mother Rose who lived in Lambeth, and the fact he paid her an allotment (or allowance) of 5s a week from his wages. There is also a note that the Admiralty promised to send Mrs Fowler a copy of his death certificate.

Prisoners of War

Apart from some papers in ADM 1, ADM 116 and ADM 137, with an index to correspondence in ADM 12 (code 79), there are no unique records for naval prisoners of war. For more about prisoners of war see Chapter 4.

The records are discussed in more detail in Sarah Paterson, *Tracing Your Prisoner of War Ancestors, the First World War*, Pen & Sword, 2012.

Medals and Awards

Naval personnel were entitled to the same campaign medals as their military counterparts. Rolls for these medals are in ADM 171 and online through Ancestry: but they are much less informative than the Army medal index cards. They contain the individual's name, rank and on occasion specialism, whether he was in the RNR or RNVR, any gallantry medals awarded, but generally entries are B and V for British War and Victory medals, and where the medals were despatched, normally S for sent or the name of the ship the recipient was on. Occasionally, there is an additional note, the meaning of which has almost always been lost.

Incidentally, Findmypast includes transcriptions of the cards for officers by Jack Marshal, which is rather easier to use and understand than the original.

ADM 171 also contains brief details of medals awarded for gallantry. A full list of men who received gallantry medals can be found at http://naval-history.net. It is taken from entries in the *London Gazette*. It is arranged by medal and then by date the medal was gazetted. Again, captains' reports may well include recommendations for gallantry medals.

Operational Records

It can be frustratingly difficult to track down reports and descriptions of naval activities during the First World War.

Ships' logbooks (in ADM 53, with submarine logs in ADM 173) normally only include weather and navigational details. Perhaps of more immediate use are the brief histories of most ships which are available at www.battle-ships-cruisers.co.uk/royal.htm. It is also worth checking to see whether there is an entry for the ship in Wikipedia. A project to put ships' logs for the war period online is at www.oldweather.org.

Records relating to actions fought by ships or planning by the Admiralty might be found in three other series (in order of usefulness ADM 137, ADM 116 and ADM 1), although a search of TNA's Catalogue may well be able to identify the correct place to start. For example, ADM 137/10 contains papers about the naval campaign in the early months of the war and the loss of HMS *Pegasus* in September 1914.

THE COASTGUARD

Service records for Coastguards, many of whom had served in the Navy up to 1923, are in ADM 175. Unfortunately, there is no index, so you have to know roughly when and where your ancestor served. During the First World War many men were awarded campaign medals, which are listed in the naval medal rolls on Ancestry.

Royal Marines

During the First World War the Marines were divided into RM Light Infantry and RM Artillery. Both served on land (as part of the RND) and at sea. Probably their greatest feat of bravery was the dramatic raid on the German submarine pens at Zeebrugge on St George's Day 1918 during which two members received the Victoria Cross.

RM officers' records (including warrant officers) are in series ADM 196 (available through TNA's Online Records Service), and these give full details of service and include, in some cases, the name and profession of the officer's father. Officers are also listed in both the Navy and Army Lists.

Service records for Marines are in ADM 159, which provide a Marine's date and place of birth, trade, physical description, religion, date and place of enlistment and a full record of service with comments on conduct. These are available through TNA's Online Records Service. In addition, there are attestation papers in ADM 157, which are loose forms, compiled for each Marine on enlistment. They give birthplace, previous occupation, physical description and often a record of service. Lance Corporal William Robert Mitchell was a mason's labourer when he joined up in September 1904, aged 18. During the war he had served on board the *Neptune* and *Royal Sovereign*, before being sent to France on 17 April 1917. On 26 October 1917 there is the final entry 'D assumed dead' in his service record (ADM 159/153)which alludes to the fact that he was posted missing and his name can be found on the memorial to the missing at Tyne Cot.

Many service records for men who served in the Chatham, Deal and Plymouth Divisions (but not Portsmouth) during the First World War are at the FAAM.

Awards of campaign and gallantry medals are in the naval medal index cards in series ADM and online at Ancestry. But perhaps of more use are the transcriptions of the cards for the Marines by Jack Clegg, available through Findmypast. PLY//13203 Lance Corporal W R Mitchell's medals went to the Universal Legatee, that is the person (not necessarily the next of kin) to whom the deceased left his estate. Marine casualties are listed alphabetically in pieces ADM 242/7-10 (and again through Findmypast), giving name, rank, number, ship's name, date and place of birth, cause of death, where buried and next of kin. Some war diaries for Marine units serving with the Army are in WO 95.

In addition, some material is held at Royal Marines Museum, Southsea PO4 9PX, www.royalmarinesmuseum.co.uk.

Further Reading

There are two excellent websites about the RN during the First World War: www.worldwar1.co.uk and www.naval-history.net. An excellent, if idiosyncratic, introduction to the tangled network of naval volunteer units is at www.barnettmaritime.co.uk/reserves.htm#mmr. TNA also has some useful In-Depth Guides on its website on various aspects of researching naval personnel.

Simon Fowler, *Tracing Your Naval Ancestors*, Pen & Sword, 2011.

Bruno Pappalardo, *Tracing your Naval Ancestors*, Public Record Office, 2003.

Richard Brooks and Matthew Little, *Royal Marine Ancestors*, Pen & Sword, 2008.

Ken Divall, *Tracing Royal Marine Ancestors*, SOG, 2007.

Merchant Navy

In 1914 Britain had the largest merchant fleet in the world. British-owned and crewed ships could be found in every port around the world. The war took a heavy toll, with thousands of tons of shipping lost largely to German submarines; and 14,287 seamen lost their lives. Crew members came from all over the world with significant numbers of Indians and West and East Africans. Indeed, only 60 per cent of the men who died were British born. Virtually all officers, including the author's paternal grandfather, however, were British.

Service Records

Service records for men who served in the Merchant Navy during the First World War are almost non-existent. And those which do are complicated to use. Fortunately, there are some excellent Research Guides on TNA's website which explain these records in detail. Len Barnett also offers sage advice about tracing merchant seamen at www.barnettmaritime.co.uk/main.htm.

Record cards from the Central Index Register for ordinary seamen who served between 1913 and 1920 were destroyed some time ago. All that survives are the cards for 270,000 seamen from a special index for 1918 to 1921 (series BT 350). Each card usually gives name, place and date of birth, a short description and a photograph of the man. A set is online on Findmypast. Incomplete online databases extracted from these cards for men who were born in Ireland are at www.irishmariners.ie and for those born in Wales at www.welshmariners.org.uk.

Agreements and crew lists show which men served on individual ships: a separate document was completed for each voyage. As the record cards for the war years are missing these are the only reliable source of information about an ancestor's service on merchant ships. TNA has a 10 per cent sample in BT 99, with an index to the ships in the Open Reading Room. Those for 1915 are with the NMM. Lists for ships registered in Belfast are with the Public Record Office of Northern Ireland and those at Dublin in the National Archives of Ireland. The remainder (80 per cent of the total) are with the Maritime History Archive, Memorial University of Newfoundland, St John's, NL, A1C5S7, Canada (www.mun.ca/mha). Their Crew Lists Index Search page is at www.mun.ca/mha/holdings/searchcrew.php. You need the ship's Official Number to search. There are some indexes on the website of the Crew List Index Project (www.crewlist.org.uk), which in theory end in 1913, although there is some material for later periods. Otherwise, it is a matter of finding Lloyd's Registers which will provide the information. Sets are held at TNA, the Guildhall Library in London (where Lloyd's records are kept) and other maritime archives. The Maritime History Archive will photocopy the appropriate documents for you for a small charge.

Ship's logs contain details of a man's conduct on board and whether he became sick or died during the voyage. A very large collection can be found in BT 165.

Casualties

There are number of different sources that can be used. The best place is probably the CWGC (www.cwgc.org). The names of those who have no known grave are inscribed on the Tower Hill Memorial which lies opposite Tower Underground station in London.

Another source is S B and D B Jarvis, *The Cross of Sacrifice: Officers, Men and Women of the Merchant Navy and Mercantile Fleet Auxiliary, 1914–1919*, Naval & Military Press, 2003. For each entry the name of the ship the individual served on is given, with the date it sank, and the individual's function on board, such as master, mate, stewardess, greaser, trimmer or fireman.

The NMM has returns of deaths between 1914 and 1919; and at TNA there are the Registers of Deceased Seamen, 1914–18 (BT 334/62, 65, 67, 71 and 73) with a roll of honour in BT 339.

The Merchant Navy Association, PO Box 35, Torpoint PL11 2WD (www.mna.org.uk) may also be able to help. The archive has complete records of all merchant seamen who lost their lives during wartime (full name, rating, ship, date and often age and home town), records of their

An artist's drawing of the war memorial to the men of the Merchant Navy on Tower Hill. (Author's collection)

ships, how their ships were lost (cause of loss, U-boat details, time and place of attack, voyage and cargo, references to official records and much more). A charge, currently £50, is made for checking these records. However, much of this data can be found online for free.

Prisoners of War

A number of lists of merchant seamen and fishermen held prisoner by the Germans are in FO 383 with a detailed description of the series available through TNA's Catalogue. There is also a list of men taken prisoner in 1916 and 1917 in MT 9/1098.

The most famous merchant seaman prisoner of war was Captain Charles Fryatt. During the First World War the Great Eastern Railway maintained its steamer services from Britain to the Netherlands, despite the dangers posed by German naval forces. Captain Fryatt captained the *Brussels*, which regularly sailed from Harwich to the Hook of Holland. In 1915 he escaped the threat of capture by the German *U-33*. Refusing to obey its order to stop, he steamed straight towards it, forcing it to submerge. The German authorities regarded this as an act of piracy, outside the laws of war, and they had not forgotten about it when the *Brussels* and her crew fell into their hands in July 1916. Fryatt was tried by court martial for trying to sink the *U-33* and summarily executed. This was used by the British as another example of German 'frightfulness'. At the end of the war Fryatt's body was exhumed and after a ceremony at St Paul's Cathedral was buried in Dovercourt cemetery in Harwich. TNA has some records, including the Agreement and Crew List for the ship (BT 99/3210) and a claim for pension from his widow, the entry in TNA's Catalogue says 'Nature of Disability or Cause of Death: Shot' (PIN 26/19752).

Operational Records

It can be difficult to find very much about individual ships during the war. Lists of those that sunk, with brief details of when, where and how they were lost, can be found at www.naval-history.net/WW1LossesBrMS1917 .htm. Gordon Smith, who runs the site, is compiling a more detailed list, although at time of writing it only covers the early months of the war. Slightly fuller records can be found at www.mariners-l.co.uk/ WWI%20LOSSES%20INDEX.htm. Also useful is the superb U-Boat.Net website which contains much about attacks on Allied ships by German U-boats. It is mainly about the Second World War, but there is a comprehensive section dealing with the First World War at www.uboat.net/ww1, where you can find out more about ships lost and who sank them.

The information is, however, largely based on the official *British Vessels Lost at Sea 1914–1918*, which was published in 1919, with copies in MT

LND I MION, sailing vessel, 67grt, 30 March 1917, English Channel, reportedly sunk by submarine, not known how sunk, 4 lives lost including Master

BRODNESS, 5,736grt, defensively-armed, 31 March 1917, 5 miles WNW from Port Anzio, torpedoed without warning and sunk by submarine,

BOAZ, sailing vessel, 111grt, 31 March 1917, 15 miles NE from C Barfleur, captured by submarine, sunk by bombs

PRIMROSE, sailing vessel, 113grt, 31 March 1917, 35 miles SE from Start Point, sunk by submarine gunfire, 1 life lost

GIPPESWIC, sailing vessel, 116grt, 31 March 1917, 15 miles NE from C Barfleur, captured by submarine, sunk by bombs

BRAEFIELD, 427grt, 31 March 1917, Bristol Channel, possibly torpedoed without warning and sunk by submarine, date uncertain, listed as 31st?, 10 lives lost including Master

COONAGH, 1,412grt, March 1917, English Channel, sunk by submarine but not known how, listed in March, 10 lives lost including Master

ACTON, 207grt, 31 March 1917, English Channel, SubmarineNot knownNot known, date not known, listed in March, 6 lives lost including Master

APRIL 1917

WARREN, 3,709grt, defensively-armed, 1 April 1917, 20 miles SW from Civita Vecchia, torpedoed without warning and sunk by submarine, 3 lives lost Master made prisoner

KASENGA, 4,652grt, defensively-armed, 1 April 1917, 2 miles from the Hormigas, Cape Palos, torpedoed without warning and sunk by submarine,

EASTERN BELLE, sailing vessel, 97grt, 1 April 1917, 30 miles SW from St Catherine's Point, captured by submarine, sunk by bombs

SILVIA, sailing vessel, 164grt, 1 April 1917, 15 miles SSE from the Owers LV, captured by submarine, sunk by bombs

A list of merchant shipping lost on 30 March 1917. (Naval-History.Net)

25/83-85. There are one or two Courts of Enquiry in BT 369 and occasionally papers may be found in ADM 137. Outside TNA, Lloyd's Marine Collection, at the Guildhall Library in London, may well have material.

There are official registers and related paperwork for shipping that are a bit outside the scope of this guide. Brief records, seemingly for every ship throughout the First World War, together with an idea of where you can find more information, is provided by Crew List Index Project at www.crewlist.org.uk.

Lists of passengers going or coming to ports outside Europe and the Mediterranean are all online. Those for passengers leaving Britain are on Findmypast, while Ancestry has those for people arriving in Britain. They do not include troopships, although occasionally you may find listed small parties of officers or soldiers going or coming to India or the Colonies. You can also trace relations and family members coming and going to Britain, for example, my grandfather's return from Japan in early 1915 and the precipitous departure to South Africa of the widow of Lieutenant Eric Rogers MC after his death in September 1916.

Medals and Awards

Men of the Mercantile Marine Reserve, and officers and men of the RNR, received the 1914–15 Star (if they had seen service before the end of 1915),

The Merchant Marine medal and the envelope it came in which was awarded to my grandfather Paul Belcher Fowler. (Author's collection)

the British War Medal and the Victory Medal. The Mercantile Marine Medal was also awarded to those with sea service of not less than six months between 4 August 1914 and 11 November 1918, and who served at sea on at least one voyage through a danger zone. All those who received the Mercantile Marine Medal were automatically entitled to receive the British War Medal, and cards for recipients can be viewed on TNA's Online Records Service (series BT 351) and list the medals issue, service number and the individual's date of birth, but not any of the ships he served on.

Merchant seamen were entitled to several unique medals for gallantry, generally awarded for saving lives. The highest award was the Albert Medal, for which there will be an announcement and citation in the *London Gazette*. Lists of recipients are at www.marionhebblethwaite.co.uk/gcindex.htm and www.naval-history.net/WW1MedalsBr-AM.htm. There should also be files about the award to individuals in HO 45 and MT 9 at TNA. Interestingly, the Home Office files include papers for men who were nominated for the award, but who did not receive it for one reason or

The authorisation to wear the medal sent to my grandfather by the Board of Trade. It contains the same information as appears on the medal cards available on TNA's Online Records Service. (Author's collection)

another. Registers of men awarded the Sea Gallantry Medal are in BT 261. Again, there should be an announcement in the *London Gazette*.

Other Sources

Shipping companies often kept records of their employees. However, many companies amalgamated or were taken over by rivals, particularly after the Second World War. The NRA should be able to tell you which records are available where; it is available online at www.nation-alarchives.gov.uk/nra.

Many merchant seamen and their officers served in the RNR, so it is worth checking their records as well (see above).

Further Reading

There are several guides to researching merchant seamen ancestors:
Kelvin Smith et al., *Records of Merchant Seamen and Shipping*, Public Record Office, 1998.
William Spencer, *Medals: The Research Guide*, TNA, 2006.

Chris and Michael Watts, *My Ancestor was in the Merchant Navy*, SOG, 2004.

Michael Wilcox, *Fishing and Fishermen: a Guide for Family Historians*, Pen & Sword, 2009.

Simon Wills, *My Ancestor was a Merchant Seaman*, Pen & Sword, 2013.

As well as the websites mentioned above, some information can be obtained from the Mariners website at www.mariners-l.co.uk, although the section on the First World War could do with being updated and it is not easy to navigate your way around.

Chapter 6

IN THE AIR

T
he RAF is by far the youngest of the services, being formed as late as 1 April 1918. The new service had its origins in the Balloon Section of the Royal Engineers, which was established in 1879 to provide reconnaissance balloons for use in colonial campaigns and later in the Boer War. Yet, flying of heavier than air machines in Britain was slow to develop. The American showman 'Colonel' Samuel F. Cody made the first flight in Britain as late as 16 October 1908 at Farnborough. The military planners were, however, less than impressed with this new technology. In a report for the Committee of Imperial Defence in 1909 Lord Esher recommended that the Navy be allowed £35,000 to build an experimental airship and the Army £10,000 for experiments on navigable balloons. Esher, however, saw 'no necessity for the Government to continue experiments in aeroplanes provided that advantage is taken of private enterprise in this form of aviation'. One example of this was the training undertaken by the Royal Aero Club on behalf of the Army. Successful students had their fees refunded on their joining the Royal Flying Corps (RFC).

The RFC itself was formed in 1912, combining existing Army and Navy flying activities. In July 1914, the naval wing broke away to become the Royal Naval Air Service (RNAS): wags claimed that the abbreviation stood for 'Really Not A Sailor'. On the outbreak of war a month later the 4 squadrons of the RFC, totalling 105 officers (including Lieutenant Vivian Wadham), 63 aeroplanes and 95 lorries, were sent to France. Left at home were 116 aircraft (described as 'mainly junk'), 41 officers and a few hundred airmen.

The First World War saw a rapid expansion in the air services and the work undertaken by aircraft. The RFC spent much of its time offering support to the Army on the Western Front and elsewhere by initially operating reconnaissance missions, and later through artillery spotting and bombing German targets in Belgium. Until February 1916 the RNAS was responsible for the air defence of Britain (when responsibility was transferred to the RFC), and was the pioneer of strategic bombing against Germany and sites in occupied Belgium from its base in Dunkirk. In addition, the service operated patrols from coastal air stations in Britain and from ships, including by 1918 the first aircraft carriers.

The mobility and freedom of the air was often contrasted with the stalemate of the trenches, particularly by the media. Even so the life of pilots and observers was usually merry and generally short. In 1917 the life expectancy of a pilot on the Western Front was between eleven days and three weeks. That is if they survived the brutal period of training. Of the 14,000 pilots and aircrew in the RFC who were killed, well over half lost their lives in training. One of whom was 22-year-old Lieutenant Henry Pillow, 7 Squadron RFC, who was killed on 8 August 1917, probably in a collision with another aircraft. He had been out in France for three weeks. His commanding officer wrote to his mother that: 'Your son had not been with us very long, but in that time he has shown himself as a very promising and capable pilot, who always did his work well, and he endeared himself to all he came in contact with.' (WO 339/58909).

One man who survived these long odds – only to die in the Spanish Flu pandemic a week after the Armistice – was Lieutenant Colonel Leoline Jenkins (1891–1918). He is buried in Acton cemetery in West London. Before the war Jenkins had been a schoolmaster at his old prep school at Durlston Court, Swanage in Dorset. He joined the RFC in 1915 and was posted to 15 Squadron in France just before Christmas that year. During 1916 and 1917 he flew many missions, winning the Distinguished Service Order (DSO) and the Military Cross (MC) and bar (that is a second award of the medal). A friend wrote of him:

He used to fly alone (from preference), put as much armoured protection as he could on his plane and then after flying high, swoop down like a hawk close to the German guns . . . I suppose that after the experiences of being potted at by small boys' questions in the close range of a Durlston classroom, the bullets of the Huns are of minor consequences. There is not much of the 'Wait and See' about L.J.

Unfortunately, neither the RFC nor the RNAS were particularly successful when it came to stopping German Zeppelin airship raids on British cities. Aircraft found it very difficult to locate and shoot down these huge airships. The damage caused by the raids was mainly psychological rather than actual, yet it was enough for considerable pressure to be brought upon the politicians to do something. The major problem was the lack of co-ordination between the RFC and RNAS, which was coupled with a waste of valuable resources.

Despite considerable opposition from both the Army and the Navy, a new Royal Air Force was formed on 1 April 1918 as a merger between the two air services. It was the first independent air service in the world.

RNAS squadrons had the prefix 2 or 20 added to their number, 4 RNAS Squadron, for example, became 204 Squadron. The RFC was rather larger than its naval cousin so inevitably played the dominant role, although the naval tradition of uninformative personnel records was generally adopted.

In June 1918 an Independent Force was established with the sole purpose of bombing strategic targets in Germany and a number of raids were carried out. By November 1918 the RAF had 188 squadrons, with 22,467 aircraft and 103 airships on strength, and 27,000 officers and 264,000 other ranks including 25,000 women.

AIR 1

The majority of RFC, RNAS and RAF records are at TNA and are found in one series, AIR 1, which originally was assembled by the Air Historical Branch in the 1920s for the official history of the War in the Air. As a result, it is a hotchpotch of material with many gems and, frankly, some rubbish. You just never know what you are going to find. For many units there are short histories produced shortly after the Armistice, generally prepared by the squadron adjutant, which should list officers and men who won gallantry medals, the aircraft flown and perhaps the bases where they flew from.

Unfortunately, the series is not particularly easy to use. In particular (and most unusually), you need to use the former Air Historical Branch (AHB) reference as well as the TNA piece number when you order a document. So if, for example, you want to look at a file of an airman who won the Victoria Cross you need to use both the piece number (AIR 1/519) and the AHB number (16/9/1). However, the process is a little unnecessary as readers are normally presented with the whole box not just the specific file ordered.

COMMON SOURCES

There are several resources that cover the RAF as well as the other services, and these include:

- The *London Gazette*, which records the promotion and, to a degree, postings of officers as well as the award of gallantry medals (see Chapter 3).

- The CWGC records the death of RAF personnel (see Chapter 2). In particular, the Arras Flying Services Memorial in the Faubourg-D'Amiens cemetery in northern France commemorates nearly 1,000 airmen of the RNAS, the RFC and the RAF who were killed on the whole Western Front and who have no known grave.

- Details of airmen and their officers who died during the war can be found in rolls of honour in much the same way as their Army comrades.

- For men who served before the creation of the RAF in April 1918 you should also check the sources in Chapter 3 for the Army (for the RFC) and to an extent Chapter 5 for the Navy (RNAS).

- There are medal index cards for nearly 27,000 officers and airmen (as well as 19 women) who transferred from the RFC to the RAF in April 1918. Where there is no card, exactly the same information can be found in the service records of airmen in AIR 79 (but not on officers' records in AIR 76). For more about the cards and what they can tell you, see Chapter 3.

The medal index card for Colonel Leoline Jenkins, RAF. (Ancestry/TNA WO 372)

Service Records

Officers

TNA has service records for RAF officers and airmen who were discharged before the early 1920s. It's not possible to be specific as there is no clear cut-off date. I have certainly found records for men who were serving in the mid-1920s. They include details about next of kin, civilian occupation, units in which an individual served, appointments and promotions, and honours and medals awarded. In addition, comments may have been added by training officers about the individual's flying skills or (more likely) lack of them. As might be expected, there is considerably more about pilots, navigators and observers than for the engineering staff who maintained the aircraft or the clerical staff working behind the scenes. The records are all available through the TNA's Online Records Service.

It can sometimes be difficult to work out from the service record what an officer's job was. Lieutenant John Swain, for example, was a member of 70 Squadron in 1918, but because of a previous gunshot wound he was

A page of the service record for Lieutenant John Swain, RAF. (TNA AIR 76/492)

certainly not a pilot, but what he did is not clear from his service record (AIR 76/492). As he attended an Armaments School in late 1917, he may have been the Squadron's Armament Officer, but this is just a guess.

Later service records are with the MoD. More details can be found at www.veterans-uk.info.

The RAFM also holds medical board record cards for officers between 1917 and about 1920. These cards record attendance at medical boards and the boards' findings for RFC and RAF officers. For RFC officers this duplicates material that should appear in their service records in WO 339 or WO 374.

For pilots it is worth looking at the Royal Aero Club Aviators' Certificates on Ancestry, which contains approximately 28,000 index cards and 34 photograph albums of aviators who were issued with their flying licences by the Royal Aero Club mainly between 1910 and late 1915 when the RFC and RNAS began to train their own pilots. The cards include name, birth date, birthplace, nationality, rank or profession, date and place of certificate, and certificate number. One of the first was Vivian Wadham, originally a second lieutenant in the Hampshire Regiment. His card notes he trained at the Sopwith School at Brooklands, Surrey on a Farman biplane and passed on 16 July 1912. There is also a photograph of a determined looking young man.

The squadron records in AIR 1 are particularly good for pilots and navigators and officers. But what is available varies greatly between units. For

---

1423

JENKINS, Leoline
  Royal Flying Corps, South Farnborough,
                                          Hants.

Born 3rd May, 1891.   at   Plymouth
Nationality British
Rank or Profession   Captain R.G.A.
Certificate taken on   Maurice Farman Biplane
At Military School, Farnborough
Date   6th July, 1915.

The Royal Aero Club's record of the pilot's licence awarded to Leoline Jenkins. (Ancestry/Royal Aero Club/RAFM)

70 Squadron, for example, the records are largely for officers who were serving in the unit in the early months of 1919. However, for 7 Squadron RFC, for example, details of the officers (and airmen) who were killed are to be found in the squadron history, which confirms that Lieutenant Pillow died on 8 August 1917 and indicates that his navigator, who was also killed, was Aircraftsman H V Bennetto (AIR 1/687/21/20/7).

On the formation of the RAF a new Air Force List was published along the lines of the Army and Navy Lists with brief details of officers. The only copy that TNA has for the period of the First World War is for April 1918, but the RAFM and IWM may have other issues. The April 1918 issue is also available online at TheGenealogist.

Other Ranks

Records of RAF other ranks are in AIR 79. They are arranged in service-number order. Apart from personal details, these records include dates of

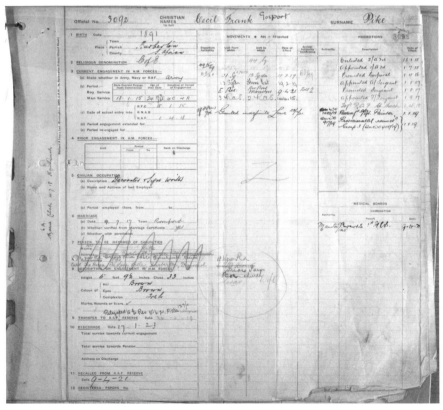

A page from the service record of 3092 Sergeant Cecil Pike, RAF. (TNA WO 79/39)

enlistment and discharge, promotions and units served with, brief notes of medical and disciplinary history (like the Navy there is often a mark for character) and dates of service overseas. In addition, they contain the same information as the medal index cards, so if there isn't an actual card for your man, this is a more than adequate alternative.

The indexes are on microfilm in the Open Reading Room at TNA, although you have to order the records themselves which are arranged in service-number order. It is likely that these will be online by 2014. In addition, records for airmen who stayed in the RAF after 1920 or who served between the wars, may be transferred to TNA shortly.

AIR 79 also includes some service papers for men who joined the RFC, but who for one reason or another did not join the RAF. Perhaps they had died in the service, like 2nd Class Air Mechanic Bennetto who was killed with Lieutenant Pillow, or were later commissioned as an officer, as happened to 3090 F/Sgt Charles Cunningham Gissing in March 1918 (AIR 79/39).

In addition, TNA has two copies of a muster roll of all other ranks compiled in early April 1918 arranged in service-number order. It is also available on Findmypast. The muster will tell you what the man's trade was, when he joined the RFC or was promoted and his daily pay. However, the muster will not indicate which unit he belonged to.

Other ranks who joined the RFC between its formation in 1912 and August 1914 (numbers 1–1400), are described in some detail in J V Webb and I McInnes, *The Contemptible Little Flying Corps*, London Stamp Exchange, 1991. TNA library has a copy of the book and a reprint is available from Naval & Military Press.

ROYAL NAVAL AIR SERVICE

The Navy wing broke away from the Royal Flying Corps a few weeks before the outbreak of the First World War and became the Royal Naval Air Service. The new service had 93 aircraft, 6 airships, 2 balloons and 727 personnel.

During the First World War the main roles of the RNAS were fleet reconnaissance, patrolling coasts for enemy ships and submarines, attacking enemy coastal territory and defending Britain from enemy air raids, along with deployment along the Western Front. There was, however, continued inter-service rivalry with the RFC which led to wastage in aircraft and other resources. But more seriously for the politicians the division had a big impact on the air defence of Britain itself. Neither force seemed able to combat German air attacks. It was agreed to merge the two services. On 1 April 1918 the RNAS, which at this time had 67,000 officers and men, 2,949 aircraft, 103 airships and 126 coastal stations, joined with the RFC to form the Royal Air Force.

A brief history of the RNAS is at www.theaerodrome.com/services/gbritain/rnas/index.php.

Service records for other ranks in the RNAS who did not transfer to the RAF (or who had died or been invalided out before 1 April 1918) are in ADM 188 and can be searched in the normal way (see Chapter).

Officers' records are in ADM 273. They are arranged by service-number order, although there is an index available through TNA's Catalogue. The records will give you details of which units an individual served with, next of kin and often candid comments by superior offices about performance and conduct. Entries will indicate whether an individual transferred to the RAF or not.

Information about the officers and ratings of the RNAS who died during the war are in series ADM 242 (and online through Findmypast). In addition, S D and D B Jarvis, *The Cross of Sacrifice: Officers who Died in the Service of the RN, RNVR, RM, RNAS and RAF, 1914–1919*, Naval & Military Press, 2000, describes the careers of RNAS and RAF officers who died on active service during the war.

Reports and other operational records for the RNAS are in ADM 137. Diaries (known as line books) describing the activities of many RNAS units are with the FAAM.

FLIGHT MAGAZINE

Launched in 1909, *Fight* has covered the whole history of British aviation almost since its inception. Copies of the magazine between 1909 and 2005 are online at www.flightglobal.com/pdfarchive/index.html. If you have an ancestor who was a pilot or otherwise a senior figure in the air services, it is worth checking to see if there is anything about him (or her) here. Unfortunately, however, the search engine isn't terribly good at narrowing down searches so you have to do a bit of casting about to find anything.

Casualties

The IWM has a roll of honour for members of the RFC and RNAS who died during the war. Both the RAFM and the IWM have copies of G C Campbell's *Royal Flying Corps: Casualties and Honours during the War 1914–1917*, which list pilots and navigators (officers only) who died between 1914 and 1917. Entries can be very informative, and a typical one reads:

Captain Vivian Hugh Nicholas Wadham RFC. and 1st Btn Hampshire Regiment killed in action in Flanders over the German lines on February 17th 1916 was aged 24, eldest son of Mr and Mrs Hugh D. Wadham of Thamesfield Shepperton-on-Thames. He entered the Hampshire Regiment from the Special Reserve in June 1914 and was promoted lieutenant in the following December. In May he was appointed flight commander in the Military Wing of the RFC, with the temporary rank of Captain.

This can be a useful source as airmen and officers do not appear in Soldiers Died in the Great War.

Brief details of the service of NCOs and men appears in S B and D B Jarvis, *The Cross of Sacrifice: Non-Commissioned Officers, Men and Women of the UK, Commonwealth and Empire Who Died in the Service of the Royal Naval Air Service, Royal Navy, Royal Marines, Royal Flying Corps and Royal Air Force 1914–1921*, Naval & Military Press, 1996, and Chris Hobson, *Airmen Died in the Great War 1914–1918; The Roll of Honour of the British and Commonwealth Air Services of the First World War*, Naval & Military Press, 1998.

Reports of aircraft (and pilot) casualties on the Western Front between March 1916 and April 1919 are in AIR 1/843-860, 865, with other lists in AIR 1/914-916, 960-969. The RAFM holds an extensive set of record cards relating to deaths, injuries and illnesses suffered by RFC and RAF personnel (and former members of the RNAS after 1 April 1918). They cover the period roughly between 1915 and 1928. These cards cover circumstances from off-duty sporting accidents to deaths. The records are not complete but a variable amount of information can be gleaned from them. Some cards record the movements of prisoners of war or give Court of Enquiry summaries for accidents occurring in Britain. Details recorded for other ranks are usually much briefer than those for officers. Serial numbers and types of aircraft are sometimes given. The cards are being digitised at present and should be online in 2014.

Operational Records

There are several series of operational records that can help illustrate a man's career in the RFC, RNAS and RAF.

The Air Services issued daily and fortnightly communiqués for the use of the press, which may give an idea of what was happening in the air day by day. Both the RAFM and TNA have incomplete sets and they have been published. A typical one is for 31 March 1917:

A reconnaissance of the 1st Brigade observed fires in Lievin, Willerval and one mile east of Roclincourt. Considerable train movement was seen behind Queant and Baralle in the early morning. A large explosion was observed at Crosilles and fires were seen burning in Pronville, Queant and in other places.

Artillery co-operation 28 targets were dealt with by aeroplane observation. Artillery of the First Army obtained four direct hits on hostile batteries. Three gun pits were destroyed and three explosions were caused. One of which was very large.

Artillery of the Third Army obtained 13 direct hits on hostile batteries, and damaged gun emplacements. Seven direct hits were obtained on trenches.

Hostile aircraft – Major AJL Scott, Squadron Commander 60 Squadron destroyed a hostile machine south-east of Arras, Captain CT Black, 60 Squadron assisted Major Scott. A second hostile aeroplane was destroyed NE of Arras by Lieutenant WA Bishop, 60 Squadron. A patrol of three Nieuports, 29 Squadron, drove down a hostile machine out of control in the vicinity of Gavrelle. Two other German machines were forced to land after having been engaged by Lieutenants Binnie and WE Molesworth both of 60 Squadron. (TNA AIR 1/2116/204/57)

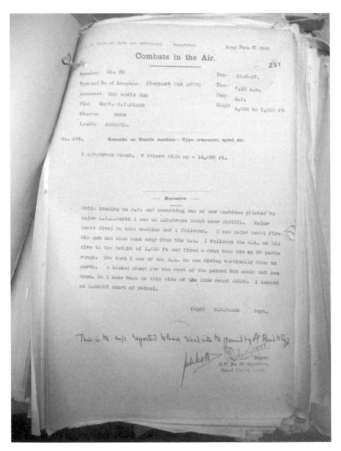

A combat report submitted by Lt W A Bishop of 60 Squadron RFC recording the shooting down of a German plane near Arras on 31 March 1917. (TNA AIR 1/225/204/5/2634 pt 1)

For many squadrons, and occasionally for other units, there are operational record books which give some idea of what happened day by day, although they are rarely as informative as their Second World War equivalents.

There may also be other records that can shed light on a man's career as a pilot or navigator, such as lists of property forwarded to next of kin or combat reports compiled after a German aircraft had been shot down.

Combat reports are particularly valuable, although they should be treated with some caution, as pilots tended to claim planes that they had not shot down. The British, for example, claimed over 7,000 victories from June 1916 to the Armistice, yet German records show they only lost 3,000 aircraft. They are arranged by Squadron and can be found in AIR 1. On 31 March 1917, Captain C T Black, 60 Squadron RFC, compiled one such report:

> While leading an OP [observation post] and escorting one of our machines piloted by Major A R Scott I saw an Albatross Scout over Hesinil. Major Scott dived on this machine and I followed. I saw Major Scott fire his gun and then bank away from the HA [hostile aircraft] I followed the HA on his dive to the height of 1000 feet and fired a drum unto him at 50 yards range. The last I saw of the HA he was diving vertically down to earth. I looked about for the rest of the patrol but could not find them, so I came back on this side of the line around Arras. I landed at Larbret short of petrol. (TNA AIR 1/225/204/5/2634 pt 1)

A few pilots' logbooks are at TNA (look in AIR 4 for aircraft and AIR 3 for airships), but the RAFM has a larger collection.

There are a number of published squadron histories and websites dedicated to individual units, which are well worth checking out.

Medals and Awards

It can be difficult to find information about gallantry awards made to RFC, RNAS and RAF personnel. They are gazetted in the *London Gazette* (www.london-gazette.co.uk), but rarely contain citations. There are, however, a few unindexed files containing citations that were presented to the King for his formal approval in series AIR 2 (code 30).

The RNAS equivalents are in ADM 171/89-91, 94-119 and online on Ancestry. In using these records it may help to know that RNAS personnel were technically on the strength of HMS *Pembroke* until 2 February 1915 when they were transferred to HMS *President*.

Further Reading

William Spencer, *Air Force Records for Family Historians*, 2nd edn, TNA, 2008.

Phil Tomaselli, *Tracing Your RAF Ancestors*, Pen & Sword, 2009.

The war service of many pilots, particularly those regarded as 'aces' (that is those who shot down five or more enemy aircraft), has been researched and published in books, such as C F Shores, N L R Franks and R Guest, *Above the Trenches. A Complete Record of the Fighter Aces and Units of the British Empire Air Forces, 1915–1920*, Naval & Military Press, 1990, with a supplement in 2002, and for bomber crews their *Above the War Fronts: A Complete Record of the British Two Seater Bomber Pilot and Observer Aces, the British Two-Seater Fighter Observer*, Naval & Military Press, 1997.

Surprisingly, there seems to be no authoritative website devoted to British military aviation during the First World War, although both www.theaerodrome.com and www.wwiaviation.com may be of use. Cross and Cockade is a society devoted to researching the war in air and you can find out more at www.crossandcockade.com (which also has a number of useful resources).

Chapter 7

WOMEN AND CIVILIANS
AT WAR

Before the war women, apart from a few nurses and school teachers, were excluded from service in either the Army or the Navy. Traditionally, women in wartime played little role except perhaps knitting comforts for the troops. But all this would change rapidly, partly because of a shift in social attitudes, but mainly because there was an increasing shortage of manpower at home, as men had joined up. Also, women were more self-confident than they had ever been before. By the Armistice tens of thousands had joined the services to nurse, to clean and to administer. While at home hundreds of thousands worked in munitions factories, on the land or for charities.

Their reward was the vote, although initially this was only to women over 30, and the abolition of restrictions into the professions. But after the Armistice many women found that opportunities for advancement were curtailed as the men returned home and demanded their old jobs back.

Despite their contribution to the war effort, there are relatively few records for women. Before you start you will need to have a rough idea about your ancestor's war service.

WOMEN'S WAR WORK COLLECTION/WOMEN AT WORK COLLECTION

Soon after the establishment of the IWM in 1917 it was decided to collect as much as possible about the women's war effort both on the home front and within the military. By 1920 a huge range of material from posters to postcards, minutes to memoranda had been brought together. This collection is an immensely valuable resource if you want to find out more about what your grandmother or great-grandmother did during the First World War.

The collection can be consulted at the museum. It has been digitised but is only available in a few university libraries: ask for the Women, War and Society package. However, there is a useful introduction online at www.tlemea.com.

Women at War

Common Records

There are certain records that apply to all three services:

- Women who served overseas either in the forces or as a volunteer in a hospital or canteen were entitled to the same campaign medals as men. Details of these awards can be found in the medal index cards (and medal rolls) in the same way you would research a soldier or sailor. The information given is identical (see Chapter 3) However, Ancestry's set does not include women recipients so you must use those on TNA's Online Record Service.

- The appointment, promotion and resignation of officers in the nursing services and auxiliary corps should be recorded in the *London Gazette*. In addition, the *Gazette* will record the award of gallantry medals to women (generally the Royal Red Cross and MiD) and civilians (such as the Albert Medal, which was awarded for saving lives at sea, and the Edward Medal for heroism in mines and industry).

- War diaries may note the transfer of women in and out of hospitals or other units, and occasionally may include other information as well. On 29 April 1915, the war diary for No. 2 General Hospital at Le Havre recorded that Acting Sister Phyllis Pearse 'attached 10 General Hospital, Rouen died at 10am. Cause of death injuries to head, resulting from throwing herself from a window in the Officer's Hospital, while undergoing treatment for Neurasthenia [depression]' (WO 95/4074).

- Several thousand women were killed on active service. They are commemorated in the normal way by the CWGC. Miss Pearse is buried at Ste Marie Cemetery, Le Havre, along with nearly 2,000 men and women who either worked at the hospitals in the town or died of wounds while waiting to return to Britain.

- In addition, many Army workers, nurses and VADs are listed in Soldiers Died in the Great War (see Chapter 3) including some who died in Britain.

- Occasionally the names of individual women can be found on war memorials. A list also appears in *British Women's Work During the Great War with a List of Women who Died on War Service*, Imperial War Museum/Naval & Military Press, 2009 which was originally compiled for the Women's War Work Collection. The booklet also includes civilians who died in Britain and so do not appear in the Commonwealth War Graves Commission database.

Nursing

By the middle of 1917 some 45,000 nurses were serving in the armed forces and thousands more women were doing auxiliary work in hospitals at home and in France. Before the war both the Army (Queen Alexandra's

An extract from the record for Elizabeth Fowler commenting on her performance as a nurse. (TNA WO 399/2870)

Imperial Military Nursing Service (QAIMNS)) and the Navy (Queen Alexandra's Royal Naval Nursing Corps (QANNC)) had maintained small nursing services, which greatly expanded during the hostilities.

Service records for Army nurses, including members of the Territorial Force Nursing Service, are available through TNA's Online Record Service. The records can tell you where a nurse trained, references relating to their suitability as military nurses, which hospitals, Field Ambulances, Casualty Clearing Stations or other medical units they served in, confidential reports about their performance and when they left the services.

Records of nurses who served with the QAIMNS may contain details of service, enrolment and discharge papers, and correspondence relating to their period of service. The list gives forename and surname. Pension records for nurses who served with QAIMNS are in PMG 34, while records for nurses who were awarded disability pensions are in PMG 42. Piece WO 25/3956 has recommendations for the appointment of a number of nurses. A selection of medical sheets for nurses is in pieces MH 106/2207-2211.

Records for Navy nurses are in pieces ADM 104/161-165. Piece 161 is largely for nurses who joined Queen Alexandra's Royal Naval Nursing Service. The records will tell you about the hospitals a nurse served at, when they joined and left (as well as the reason for leaving). There are likely to be comments on character and performance and a note if she was awarded the Royal Red Cross. Pieces 162 to 165 are for women who joined the Queen Alexandra's Royal Naval Nursing Service Reserve for service during wartime. The records here are much less full, but you should be able to discover at which hospitals a person worked and when they joined. There are also likely to be comments on a nurse's performance. Of Nurse Janice Cunningham, who served at Haslar Naval Hospital in Gosport, it was noted, 'Does her work well, but unfortunately has a gruff and depressing manner.' (ADM 104/162 p18).

TNA has no records for members of the RAF Nursing Service. So far as is known surviving records are still with the MoD.

Nurses in general were entitled to be awarded the Royal Red Cross for meritorious service. The Royal Red Cross was created in 1883 by Queen Victoria as an award to nursing sisters or ladies for outstanding service in the care of the sick or wounded of the armed services. Just over 6,700 awards were made during the war, but often to people with little experience of nursing at the sharp end. The nursing historian Sue Light says, 'The names in the Royal Red Cross Registers held at The National Archives show that the Commandants of many voluntary hospitals, with little or no nursing training or experience, received recognition, while their staff went empty-handed.'

VADs were particularly badly treated in this respect, even though many of them endured terrible conditions and conducted themselves as bravely as their nursing colleagues. However, Helen Margaret Greatorex, who was

AUSTRALIAN ARMY NURSING
SERVICE.

Miss Nellie Frances Hill, Sister.
Miss Eleanor Wibmer Jeffries, A.R.R.C.,
Head Sister.
Miss Constance Mabel Keys, A.R.R.C., Head
Sister.
Miss Alice Joan Twynam, Head Sister.

NEW ZEALAND ARMY NURSING
SERVICE.

Miss Blanche Marion Huddleston, A.R.R.C.,
Sister.

AWARDED THE ROYAL RED CROSS.

2nd Class.

Miss Agnes Mary A'Hern, Sister,
Q.A.I.M.N.S.
Miss Martha Aitkin, Sister, T.F.N.S.
Miss Lilian Allen, Nurse, V.A.D.
Miss Mary Dorothy Allen, A./Sister,
Q.A.I.M.N.S.R.
Miss Katharine Amelia Allsop, Sister,
Q.A.I.M.N.S.
Miss Theodora Frances Almack, Nurse,
V.A.D., B.R.C.S.
Miss Margaret Rita Arnold, A./Sister, Civil
Hpl. Res.
Miss Edith Arnott, Nurse, V.A.D.
Miss Edith Gwenllian Austin, A./Sister,
Q.A.I.M.N.S.R.
Miss Mildred Isabel Austin, Sister, T.F.N.S.
Miss Amelia Ayre, A./Matron, Q.A.I.M.N.S.
Miss Margaret Dow Bain, Sister, T.F.N.S.
Miss Margaret Hendeboorcke Ballance, M.M.,
Sister, St. John's Amb. Brig.
Miss Mary Kathleen Barclay, Sister,
Q.A.I.M.N.S.
Miss Kathleen Barrett, Asst. Nurse, V.A.D.
Mrs. Mabel Katie Barr-Stevens, V.A.D. Nurse,
B.R.C.S.
Miss Grizel Gillespie Bayley, Nurse, V.A.D.
Miss Helen Margaret Bennett, Sister,
B.R.C.S.
Miss Aline Quiddington Blades, A./Sister,
Civil Hpl. Res.
Miss Margaret Janette Blake, Nurse, V.A.D.
Miss Olive Sibella Bonham-Carter, Asst.
Nurse, V.A.D.
Miss Mary Cawston Bousfield, Asst. Nurse,
V.A.D.
Miss Eliza Annie Bradshaw, Sister, T.F.N.S.
Miss Margaret Gwladys Braithwaite, Asst.
Nurse, V.A.D.
Miss Beatrice Alice Brayshaw, Sister, T.F.N.S.
Miss Mildred Breeze, A./Sister,
Q.A.I.M.N.S.R.
Miss Margaret Ethel Briggs, Sister, T.F.N.S.
Miss Janet Sinclair Bruce Brotchie, Staff
Nurse, Civil Hpl. Res.
Miss Margaret Crichton Brown, Staff Nurse,
Q.A.I.M.N.S.R.
Miss Helen Grace Brownrigg, Asst. Nurse,
V.A.D.
Miss Marjory Mitchell Bruce, Sister,
Q.A.I.M.N.S.R.
Miss Ida Doris Bull, Nurse, V.A.D., St.
John Amb. Association.
Miss Ailsa Noel Hurford Bullough, Nurse,
V.A.D.
Miss Caroline Muriel Bulteel, Sister, T.F.N.S.
Miss Eileen Mary Byrne, A./Sister, Civil Hpl.
Res.
Miss Annie MacMillan Caldwell, Nurse,
V.A.D.

Miss Mabel Copeland Capper.
Miss Lucy Kate Card, Nurse, V.A.D.
Miss Rose Carter Shaw Carleton, Sister,
Q.A.I.M.N.S.
Miss Kate Carruthers, M.M., Sister,
T.F.N.S.
Miss Hilda Clarkson, Nurse, Spec. Med. Prob.,
T.F.N.S.
Miss Caroline Mary Clements, Sister,
Q.A.I.M.N.S.R.
Miss Violet Collett, Nurse, V.A.D., St. John's
Amb. Bde.
Miss Eva Colvin, Nurse, V.A.D.
Miss Edith Elizabeth Cooke, Sister, Civil
Hpl. Res.
Miss Katie Charlotte Cooper, Sister, T.F.N.S.
Miss Cicely Gladys Cope-Morgan, Nurse,
V.A.D.
Miss May Susan Corsellis, Asst. Nurse,
V.A.D.
Miss Susanna Coulter, Sister, Civil Hpl. Res.
Miss Florence Cowper, Nurse, V.A.D.
Miss Mary Ann Cracknell, Sister, Asst.
Matron, T.F.N.S.
Miss Margaret Wilson Craig, Nurse, V.A.D.
Miss Dorothea Mary Lynette Crewdson, M.M.,
Nurse, V.A.D.
Miss Edith Winifred Croft, A./Sister,
Q.A.I.M.N.S.
The Hon. Dorothy Mary Cross, Asst. Nurse,
V.A.D.
The Hon. Georgina Marjorie Cross, Asst.
Nurse, V.A.D.
Miss Nora Cullen, Asst. Nurse, V.A.D.
Miss Mary Maitland Cunningham, Sister,
T.F.N.S.
Miss Edith Denison, Sister, T.F.N.S.
Miss Norah Creina Denny, Nurse, Spec. Med.
Probationer, attd. Q.A.I.M.N.S.
Miss Amelia Victoria Derry, Sister, T.F.N.S.
Miss Dorothy Mary Dodson, Sister, B.R.C.S.
Miss Zoë Blanche Douët, Sister, T.F.N.S.
Miss Estelle Mary Doyle, Sister,
Q.A.I.M.N.S.R.
Miss Edith Maud Drummond-Hay, Nurse,
V.A.D.
Miss Helen Sinclair Ellis, Nurse, V.A.D.
Miss Frances Georgina Fegan, Staff Nurse,
T.F.N.S.
Miss Ellen Fewlass, A./Sister,
Q.A.I.M.N.S.R.
Miss Elizabeth Young Fleming, Sister,
T.F.N.S.
Miss Millie Float, Asst. Nurse, V.A.D.
Miss Eliza Anneta Forrest, Staff Nurse,
Q.A.I.M.N.S.R.
Miss Catharine Forrestal, Asst. Nurse, V.A.D.
Miss Elizabeth Fowler, Sister,
Q.A.I.M.N.S.R.
Miss Jessie Fraser, Sister, T.F.N.S.
Miss Gladys Maud Gardiner, Nurse, V.A.D.
Miss Elsie Garner, A./Sister, Civil Hpl. Res.
Miss Elizabeth Gibson, A./Sister,
Q.A.I.M.N.S.
Miss Elsie Mabel Gladstone, A./Sister, Civil
Hpl. Res.
Miss Margaret Anne Gray, Sister, B.R.C.S.
Miss Margaret Greatorex, Nurse, V.A.D.
Miss Olive Greenwell, Nurse, Spec. Med. Pro-
bationer, T.F.N.S.
Miss Louise Griffiths, Sister, B.R.C.S.
Miss Betty Georgina Hacker, A./Sister, Civil
Hpl. Res.
Miss Sarah Hands, Sister, T.F.N.S.
Miss Mary Kathleen Harding, Nurse, V.A.D.,
St. John's Amb. Bde

Entry for Margaret Greatorex in the London Gazette *showing the award of the Royal Red Cross. (London Gazette, 3 June 1919, p. 6840)*

a VAD from Bedfordshire between April 1915 and the end of the war, was among those who was so honoured.

The decoration had two classes, first class (members) with the post nominal letters RRC and second class (associates) ARRC. Those promoted from the second to the first class returned their ARRC to the War Office. It was possible to receive bars to the RRC. Awards were announced in the *London Gazette* and there are registers in series WO 145, but they may not tell you anything you haven't already gleaned from the *London Gazette*, except the person who presented the medal, where the investiture took place and the date it happen. All this information can be found in Sue

---

May 15, 1915   **The British Journal of Nursing.**   419

institution, and all her friends and well-wishers unite in wishing her in retirement a gain to strength and happiness in the future.

She was the recipient of further handsome gifts. From Dr. and Mrs. James Macpherson Lawrie, a solid silver tea service; a gold expanding wristlet watch from her past and present Nurses; a silver cake stand from the Domestic Staff; a silver bowl from a friend.

APPOINTMENTS.

MATRON.

Royal Bath Hospital and Rawson Convalescent Home, Harrogate.—Miss F. M. Cort has been appointed Matron. She was trained at the Leeds Infirmary, and has held various appointments at the Cancer Hospital, Fulham Road, S.W., and has been Assistant Matron at the General Hospital, Nottingham.

Cottage Hospital, Potter's Bar.—Miss Florence Pitt has been appointed Matron. She was trained at the Royal County Hospital, Ryde, Isle of Wight, and has held the positions of Sister at the Royal Hospital, Richmond; Assistant Matron and Theatre Sister at Warrington Infirmary; Matron of Mold Cottage Hospital, and Matron of East Molesey Cottage Hospital, Surrey.

Convalescent Home, Stillorgan, Co. Dublin.—Miss G. D. Harley has been appointed Matron. She was trained at the London Hospital, London, and has been Night Sister and Assistant Lady Superintendent at the Royal National Hospital for Consumption, Newcastle, Co. Wicklow; also Home Sister at Sir Patrick Dun's Hospital, Dublin.

MATRON NURSE.

The Hospital, Crewkerne.—Miss Mary Dight has been appointed Matron-Nurse. She was trained at the Royal Hospital, Sheffield, and has been Sister at the Stanley Hospital, Liverpool; Matron at the Aitken Cottage Hospital, Ramsbottom, and Sister-in-Charge of the Red Cross Hospital, Ramsbottom.

SUPERINTENDENT NURSE.

Bridgwater Union.—Miss L. E. Baylis has been appointed Superintendent Nurse. She was trained at Croydon Infirmary, and has been head nurse at Sherborne Infirmary; Superintendent Nurse at Bromsgrove Infirmary, and Sister at Portsmouth Infirmary.

NIGHT SISTER.

District Hospital, West Bromwich.—Miss Ethel Eva Arnold has been appointed Night Sister. She was trained at the Princess Christian Hospital, Weymouth, where she has held the position of Sister. She has also had experience in private nursing.

SISTER.

General City Hospital, Panama (Hospital San Tomas).—Miss J. Davie has been appointed Sister. She was trained at the Seaman's Hospital,

Greenwich and the Hospital for Women, Soho Square, W.C., and has been Night Supervisor of the Children's Hospital, Nova Scotia.

CHARGE NURSE.

The Workhouse Infirmary, Sculcoates Union, Beverley Road, Hull.—Miss Annie Payne has been appointed Charge Nurse. She was trained at the North Bierley Union, Clayton, near Bradford, and is a certified midwife.

TERRITORIAL FORCE NURSING SERVICE.

Miss E. Hill, Matron, vacates her appointment (February 5th); Miss A. L. Charteris, Matron, vacates her appointment (April 1st).

LONDON COUNTY COUNCIL.

The Public Health Department of the London County Council recommended to the L.C.C. at its meeting on May 11th, subject to her fulfilling the usual requirements, that Miss Agnes Elizabeth Maud Aston be appointed a school nurse in the Public Health Department. The vacancy is caused by the resignation of Miss A. C. Proctor.

QUEEN ALEXANDRA'S IMPERIAL MILITARY NURSING SERVICE.

Miss G. Witter, to be Staff Nurse (March 30th, 1914).

QUEEN VICTORIA'S JUBILEE INSTITUTE.

TRANSFERS AND APPOINTMENTS.

Miss Elsie K. Hollway is appointed to Watford as Superintendent.

Miss Hollway received General Training at St. Thomas's Hospital, and District Training at Paddington.

Miss Mary J. Crowe is appointed to Southall-Norwood, Miss Margaret Dancey to Sevenoaks, Miss Helen E. Davies to Manchester (Ardwick), Miss Dorothy G. Jackson to Beaconsfield, Miss Victoria E. Patterson to Wolverhampton, Miss Christina B. J. Pottinger to Heanor, Miss Agnes M. Woodger to Hugglescote.

THE QUEEN ALEXANDRA RELIEF FUND FOR WAR NURSES.

The total amount received to date exceeds £10,500. Amongst the amounts are £50 from W. H. Foster, Esq.; £50 from Messrs. Smith, St. Aubyn & Company; £25 from "Anon"; and a further £36 1s., collected by Arthur Bradford, Esq.—bringing the total received through him to £1,114 7s.

The Sub-Committee are dealing with claims as they come in.

THE PASSING BELL.

PEARSE.—On April 29th, at Havre, on her way home from Rouen, Acting Sister Phyllis Pearse, Q.A.I.M.N.S., the dearly-loved younger daughter of L. F. Pearse, of 8, Eldon Park, South Norwood, aged 28 years. Buried at Havre, May 3rd, 1915.

Obituary for Phyllis Pearse in the British Journal of Nursing, *15 May 1915. (Royal College of Nursing)*

Light's indexes to the Royal Red Cross which are available on Findmypast, although these appear to be incomplete.

Using the information it may be worth seeing whether there was a story in the local newspaper about its presentation. Miss Greatorex was presented with a second class medal by the King himself at a ceremony at Buckingham Palace on 20 June 1920.

Findmypast has a small database of military nurses who were active in the early twentieth century including some 1,600 volunteers who served with the Scottish Women's Hospital. Among them is Phyllis Pearse, whose date of birth is given and father's occupation, as well as where she trained (in this case St Batholomew's Hospital) and when she joined the QAIMNS (November 1912).

The Royal College of Nursing Archives has put online copies of two journals *Nursing Record* and *British Journal of Nursing* (www.rcn.org.uk/ development/rcn_archives/historical_nursing_journals). You may well find mention of nurses in the forces, particularly if they became sisters or matrons. For Phyllis Pearse, for example, there is a short obituary in the *British Journal of Nursing* for 15 May 1915 noting that she died aged 28 at Le Havre on her way home from France, was buried on 3 May and that she was the 'dearly beloved' younger daughter of L F Pearse of South Norwood.

Voluntary Aid Detachments

The British Red Cross Society and the Order of St John had in 1909 set up a nationwide network of Voluntary Aid Detachments comprising men and women who would help in hospitals and provide other assistance on the outbreak of war. These people became known as VADs.

VADs were members either of the British Red Cross Society or the Order of St John. Both organisations kept record cards for individuals, which may include the dates of service, the nature of the duties performed, the detachment the individual belonged to, the institutions and places where the individual served and any honours that may have been awarded. In addition, there are indexes for personnel who served in military hospitals, who were trained nurses and who received the campaign medals.

Unfortunately, neither set of cards is available to researchers, although staff at both archives will do a search for you (for which they suggest a donation of £10). More details can be found at www.redcross .org.uk/About-us/Who-we-are/Museum-and-archives and the rather uninformative www.museumstjohn.org.uk/contact/index.html. Because of concerns over data protection they can only supply copies of records to the next of kin or near descendants. However, when I asked about Miss Greatorex, they helpfully supplied the following information:

> Name: Miss H Margaret Greatorex
> Detachment: Beds 12
> Rank: Nurse
> Date of Enrolment: 17/11/15
> Date of Discharge: 29/6/19
> Summary of Service: Mentioned in Despatches 30/12/18; Royal Red
> Cross 2nd class 3/6/19; France military hospital 17/4/15–29/6/19

In 1920 the British Red Cross Society awarded a medal to members of the British Red Cross or its VADs who served in Britain during the war and were therefore not eligible for British campaign medals. Those who were eligible had to have undertaken at least 1,000 hours of unpaid service, or be ambulance drivers and bearers who gave 500 hours unpaid service. No diploma was issued with the medal and it was not an official decoration. The Red Cross Archives have an alphabetical list of recipients.

Occasionally local record offices may have records. There are, for example, a fair number of photographs of groups of VADs. Probably the most complete collection, however, is at the Bedfordshire and Luton Archives Service where there are volumes of correspondence about volunteers between the county association in Bedford and the Red Cross headquarters in London. There are letters about the appointment of VADs, including Margaret Greatorex in April 1915, and two years later Florence Boyd, who wanted to become a clerk. According to a letter of 25 April 1917 from the local secretary, Miss Boyd was the daughter of a Colonel Boyd and, 'She seems a particularly nice girl and is most keen on the work. She is the very kind of member we want to get hold. I therefore trust that you will arrange that she will be posted to France as soon as possible.' (BLARS WW1/NU5). Miss Boyd was sent to a hospital in Brighton, but her medal index card suggests that she ended the war as an Assistant Administrator (that is junior officer) in the Women's Army Auxiliary Corps (WAAC). At the London Metropolitan Archives there are three volumes of reports on nurses who served in the Red Cross's London hospitals (H11/ST/C6/1-3).

Further Reading

Michelle Higgs, *Tracing Your Medical Ancestors*, Pen & Sword, 2011, offers useful advice about researching nurses.

TNA have several online Research Guides about military nurses which well summarises their holdings.

Sue Light's superb Scarlet Finders website at www.scarletfinders.co.uk/index.html has lots about military nursing during the two world wars with an emphasis on the First. She also writes a fascinating blog on nurses of the First World War at http://greatwarnurses.blogspot.com/.

Auxiliary Corps

The RN in 1916 was the first service to recruit women, who took over the role of cooks, clerks, wireless telegraphists, code experts and electricians, although it was not until November 1917 that a separate Women's Royal Naval Service (WRNS) was set up. The Army noted the success of the Navy's experiment and rather nervously established the Women's Army Auxiliary Corps (later Queen Mary's Auxiliary Army Corps (QMAAC)) in March 1917 to undertake similar work so releasing men for the front. There were widespread but almost entirely wrong concerns over morals, if young men and young women worked in close proximity, and worries over the ability of women to undertake the duties assigned them.

The WAAC was divided into four sections: Cookery; Mechanical; Clerical; and Miscellaneous. Most stayed on the home front but around 9,000 served in France. Members did not have full military status. They enrolled, they did not enlist, and breaches of discipline were dealt with by civil, not military, courts. The grades (ranks) were divided into Controllers and Administrators (officers) and Members (other ranks). Within the Members there were forewomen (sergeants), assistant forewomen (corporals) and workers (privates). Rates of pay were determined by the type of work. So, for example, a shorthand typist was paid more than a kitchen assistant. Inevitably, a member was still paid less than a man in the Army doing the same work. The WAAC uniform and accommodation were provided free but there was a weekly mess charge for food.

On the establishment of the RAF in April 1918 a separate Women's Royal Air Force (WRAF) was also set up. An attempt was made to call them penguins, as they did not fly, but the nickname did not, um, fly!

The work of the WRAF was divided into four basic trades: Clerks and Storewomen; Household; Technical; and Non-Technical. Initially, little training was given with wages based on existing experience and skills.

The majority of women were employed as clerks, with shorthand typists the most highly paid of all airwomen. Women allocated to the Household section worked the longest hours, doing back-breaking work for the lowest pay. The Technical section covered a wide range of trades, most highly skilled, including tinsmiths, fitters and welders.

WAAC

For the Army only about 9,000 records survive out of the 57,000 who served in the WAAC during the First World War. They do not include any for officials (aka officers), which may explain why there isn't one for Florence Boyd, or the several hundred members who died while with the Corps.

Their service records are surprisingly detailed with applications to join, references and correspondence about leaving, often to get married. Maud

Masey was honest enough in her resignation letter to say: 'I cannot endure this life for another five months.' (TNA WO 398/145). However, there is very little about the member's service, although the Casualty Form will indicate which units she served with and may give details of period of leave or time spent in hospital. You may find mention of the Connaught Club, which was the headquarters of the corps.

These records are at TNA in series WO 398 and online at Online Records. An incomplete nominal roll for members of the corps is in piece WO 162/16 at Kew with a list of women drivers employed during the war in WO 162/62. Recommendations for honours and awards are in WO 162/65. A selection of medical records for individual women is in series MH 106 and war diaries in pieces WO 95/84-85. The war diaries are only for units in France, but if your ancestor served overseas (and you know the unit) you may well find mention of her arrival or departure, particularly if she was an official.

An extensive collection of material relating to the QMAAC is held in the Templar Study Centre at the NAM in London (www.national-army-musuem.ac.uk), including photographs and personal papers (although no nominal rolls or service records). In addition, there is considerable material in the Women's War Work Collection at the IWM, including nominal rolls. These include officials and members, with service number, rank and full name, some also giving category and date and place of birth, date and place and cause of death.

WRNS

In the Navy about 6,000 women served in the WRNS. Service registers for officers are in series ADM 321 and a selection of personal files is in ADM 318 at TNA. Records for ratings (that is other ranks) are in ADM 336. They are all on Online Records Service. The ranks for ratings are somewhat disappointing consisting of little more than a certificate noting the ship the person served on (generally a shore base), together with a rough indication of conduct and character. Hilda Grace Fowler was an Ordinary Clerk, who served between March 1918 and October 1919 on HMS *Ceto*. Her conduct was satisfactory, character very good. The next of kin was her father Arthur Fowler, who lived in Ramsgate, which must have been convenient as *Ceto* was a depot ship based in the town's harbour. (TNA ADM 336/24). As Miss Fowler did not serve overseas she was not entitled to the British War and Victory medals. A list of women – both WRNS and nurses – who received these medals is in WO 171/133 and on Ancestry. A total of twenty-five Wrens including one officer, Evelyn Mackintosh, are officially recorded as having died, most during the influenza epidemic in the summer and autumn of 1918.

If you are researching a Wren then you may need to use the WRNS

A page from the medal roll for naval nurses. (Ancestry/TNA ADM 171/133, p. 173)

Collection at the RNM in Portsmouth (www.royalnavalmuseum.org). Although it has much more material from the Second World War than the First, it does have the original forms that ratings filled in when they enrolled. There are also collections of private papers and a selection of photographs. The NMM (www.nmm.ac.uk) in Greenwich also has a little material.

WRAF

Only records for other ranks in the WRAF survive and are to be found in series AIR 80 at TNA. No records for officers are known to survive. They are arranged alphabetically by surname and so are easy to use. They are available through the Online Records Service.

They are brief, often consisting only of the certificate of discharge on demobilisation, of which each airwoman was given a copy. This gives service number, name, rank, air-force trade, date and place of enrolment and date and place of demobilisation. It should also show age, height, build, eye and hair colour and a brief description of quality of work and personal character, signed by a WRAF officer, but sometimes not all parts are filled in.

The library at the RAFM (www.rafmuseum.org.uk) holds photographs of the WRAF at work, diaries, letters, typed accounts, badges, medals, certificates and other memorabilia.

Further Reading

Mary Ingham, *Tracing Your First World War Service Women Ancestors*, Pen & Sword, 2012 offers an excellent guide to this surprisingly complicated subject.

TNA has a selection of Research Guides on nursing and the women's auxiliary services, which describe records at Kew. In addition, the IWM has several Information Sheets on the women's auxiliary services in the Army and Navy and the VADs, which are very much based on the museum's holdings. They can be consulted at www.tlemea.com/ Resources.asp#committee.

Background

Short essays on the varying roles of women in the war based on the Women's War Work Collection at the IWM at www.tlemea.com/introduction.asp.

Civilians

Factories and Farms

As men departed for the front their places were increasingly taken by women. Approximately 1.6 million women joined the workforce in government departments, public transport, the post office, as clerks in business, as land workers and in factories, especially in the dangerous munitions factories, which employed 950,000 women by Armistice Day. They were largely young and unmarried, so had few family responsibilities.

Demobilisation certificate for Florence Paterson, who served in the WRAF. When Florence Green, as she had become, died in February 2012 she was the last known survivor of the First World War. Before her death she told a reporter that, 'I enjoyed my time in the WRAF. There were plenty of people at the airfields where I worked and they were all very good company. I met dozens of pilots and would go on dates. I had the opportunity to go up in one of the planes but I was scared of flying. It was a lovely experience and I'm very proud.' (TNA AIR 80/185)

'Munitionettes', as women workers in the munitions factories were called, were known for their unrestrained spending, for wages were high to compensate for the poor working conditions, and the peculiar yellow colour of their skins caused by the high explosives they handled.

But the most obvious change was the increasing number of women employed on buses and railways. By the end of the war about a third of all railway staff were serving in the forces; their places were very largely taken by women as cleaners, porters, station staff and clerical workers. Women were eventually to be found everywhere, although few were doing anything other than menial or relatively unskilled work.

By the end of the war 230,000 girls were working on the land, but fewer than 10 per cent were members of the Women's Land Army. The Army had been started in 1915, as the Women's Land Service Corps, to help on the land, although they faced considerable hostility from both farmers and local villagers who were suspicious of incomers.

Again, the survival of records for women employed in factories or on the land is very patchy. Certainly there are no rolls of honour (except the very partial National Roll, see below). Many records relating to the production of munitions can be found at TNA under the MUN letter code, but there is almost nothing about individual workers. Another disappointing source is the records of the Ministry of Labour in LAB 2, which are largely about trade disputes and wage agreements.

For members of the Women's Land Army there may be the occasional medal card. There may be records in the papers of local War Agricultural Committees at local record offices. Bedfordshire, in particular, has a good selection. An interesting article on the Land Army in the county is at www.galaxy.bedfordshire.gov.uk/webingres/bedfordshire/vlib/0.wla/ wla_national_world_war_one.htm.

Probably the best source is the Women's War Work Collection at the IWM. The museum holds photographs, documents, some uniform items

Members of the Women's Land Army harrowing. (Author's collection)

and first-person accounts as well as reports of national and local Agricultural Committees. County record offices and local heritage centres are worth investigating for War Agricultural Committee administrative records, Women's Land Army memorabilia and local newspaper reports.

For women (as well as men), Ancestry has some employment records, notably:

- Postal Service Appointment Books which record the date an individual was appointed, the position and place. Mrs A E Hancock (see National Roll below) was a typist appointed in 1915. There may also be additional records at the British Postal Museum and Archive, which produces an excellent guide to their genealogical resources (www.postalheritage.org.uk/page/genealogy).

- The records of most, but not all, railway companies. What you will find varies from company to company, but at least you should discover the job they did, the depot or station they worked at and when they started. Often the rate of pay is given. Once you have this it is worth looking at the railway staff magazines at TNA (under the letter code ZPER) which are full of snippets about employees either currently employed or at the front.

Otherwise the best source may be company magazines or trade journals which often include captioned photographs and lists of staff at one function or another. A typical example is the *Cocoa Works Magazine*, the works journal of Rowntrees in York which can be found at the Borthwick Institute at the University of York (www.york.ac.uk/library/borthwick).

THE NATIONAL ROLL OF THE GREAT WAR

A real oddity is the *National Roll of the Great War*, which in the words of its editor claimed, 'to supply a wonderful memorial of splendid services truly worthy of the thankful remembrance of a grateful Empire'. Unfortunately, only fourteen or so volumes were ever published for London, Southampton, Portsmouth, Bradford, Leeds, Manchester, Birmingham, Luton (and neighbouring areas), Bedford and Northampton. They are available on both Ancestry and Findmypast, although Ancestry's set is incomplete.

Each individual has an entry which briefly explains his or her war service and medals gained. Judging by how they are phrased, these entries were submitted by the individuals themselves or their families. And they probably paid a few shillings to see their war service

> HANCOCK, A. E. (Mrs.), Special War Worker.
> During the war this lady rendered valuable services in the employ of the General Post Office, and thereby released a man for military service. Her duties were carried out in an efficient manner, and she was commended for her patriotic work.
> 94, Bronsart Road, Munster Road, S.W.6   X19014B.
>
> HANCOCK, E. T., Bombardier, R.G.A.
> He joined in October, 1916, and was sent to the Western Front. He took part in many important engagements while in this theatre of war, including those at Arras, Messines Ridge, Passchendaele and Vimy Ridge. In March, 1918, during the German Offensive, he was wounded, invalided to England, and in June of the same year was discharged medically unfit for further service owing to his wounds. He holds the General Service and Victory Medals.
> 94, Bronsart Road, Munster Road, S.W.6   T19014A.
>
> HANCOCK, G., Driver, R.A.S.C. (H.T.).
> He volunteered in August, 1914, and after his training was sent to the Western Front in the same year. While in France he took an active part in many important operations, during which he was engaged on transport duties.
> In April, 1919, he obtained his demobilisation, and holds the 1914 Star, General Service and Victory Medals.
> 51, Aintree Street, Dawes Road, S.W.6   X18213.
>
> HANCOCK, R. E. G., Pte., Royal Sussex Regt.
> He joined in May, 1917, and after completing his training was drafted to India. During his two years' foreign service he was engaged on special duties at many important stations

Entry for Mrs A E Hancock in the National Roll of the Great War. Her husband is also mentioned. (Findmypast)

commemorated. By no means everybody did: neither Margaret Greatorex nor Florence Boyd who both lived in Luton did. Most entries seem to be for the lower middle or upper working classes, and the two VADs may have come from a better social strata. During the early 1920s when people began to forget the war and money was tight, fewer and fewer people subscribed so the project collapsed.

Entries can be very full and include both servicemen and civilians. Often there may be entries for both husband and wife. In Fulham, Mrs A E Hancock was a 'special war worker'. 'During the war,' her entry reads, 'this lady rendered valuable service in the employ of the General Post Office and thereby released a man for military service. Her duties were carried in an efficient manner, and she was commended for her patriotic work.' Her husband, Bombardier E T Hancock, Royal Garrison Artillery, has a detailed entry:

> joined in October 1916 and was sent to the Western Front. He took part in many important engagements while in this theatre of war including those at Arras, Messines Ridge, Passchendaele and Vimy Ridge. In March 1918, during the German offensive he was wounded and invalided to England, and in June of the same year was discharged medically unfit for medical service owing to his wounds. He holds the General Service and Victory Medals.

There is a medal card (and entry in the Silver War Badge Register), but no service record for him.

Charity Work

Although now largely forgotten, hundreds of thousands of men and, particularly, women raised millions of pounds for war charities and sent hundreds of thousands of parcels to prisoners of war. Their contribution to the war effort has almost been forgotten. More women undertook voluntary work for one or more war charity or other organisation than any other war work. Some 4 million women (about a third of the adult population) knitted garments and bandages for the troops at the front, while hundreds of thousands of others helped collect eggs to go to hospitals for wounded soldiers and sailors. Many of the ladies who helped the war charities were too old or had family commitments that prevented them from participating more actively in the war effort.

It is very difficult to find much information about individual women who were engaged in this work. Wartime charitable activity was often covered in some detail by local newspapers. These reports and occasional photographs often list the people who helped at a bazaar or members of a knitting circle. A scattering of records created by local committees can be found at local archives. In addition, TNA has details of the charities registered under the War Charities Act 1916 in series CHAR 6. These include names and addresses of individual chairmen, secretaries and treasurers.

The one exception is for the few charity workers who served in France generally running YMCA huts and refreshment buffets for soldiers. These were enormously popular facilities with the men. The volunteers were entitled to both the Victory and British War medals and their details can be found in the medal index cards on the Online Records Service. They are not available through Ancestry. Some records for the men and women who ran these huts are in the YMCA at the University of Birmingham, details at www.special-coll.bham.ac.uk.

THE ORDER OF THE BRITISH EMPIRE

The Order of the British Empire was instigated by Letters Patent on 4 June 1917. The original object was, in the words of Burke's *Handbook to the Most Excellent Order of the British Empire* (Burke Publishing Company, 1921, repr. Naval & Military Press, 2011), 'the recognition of the non-combatant war worker, who was doing his and her best to keep the fighting services working at their utmost capacity, and to look after the well-being of the fighting man at home and at the front'. In 1919 a military division to honour those in the military who had made a contribution to the war effort in ways other than by gallantry was also introduced. It had become what the *Handbook* grandly called 'democracy's own Order of Chivalry'. Inevitably, the medal was granted more to the managers and the organisers, rather than to the

133

Lady Rowley, Commandant of the Red Cross Hospital in Guildford, received the OBE for her war work. In this portrait she is wearing the Royal Red Cross. (W H Oakley, Guildford in the Great War, *Guildford, 1934, p. 91)*

actual workers themselves, but for the first time women were treated more or less on an equal footing: they received about a fifth of the total number of medals.

By the beginning of 1921 some 25,419 people had been so honoured. Military members numbered 11,369, and civilian members 13,773. Most were either Members (MBE) or Officers (OBE). The British Empire Medal (BEM) was not introduced until 1922 but, because of the passage of time, far fewer BEMs were awarded for war service.

All the original recipients are gazetted in the *London Gazette* (although the indexing, always poor, seems even worse than usual in highlighting recipients) with their full name and their job title or function, which will give some idea of why they were honoured. There should also be mention of recipients in local newspapers. Of more use, if you can get hold of a copy, is Burke's *Handbook* to the Order, which includes 'Who's Who style' entries for about two-thirds of recipients with details of their war work, along with education, occupation, home address and any clubs to which they belonged.

A not untypical example is for Lady Rowley, who was 'Vice-president of the Guildford BRCS 1910–1920, Commandant Hill House Hospital, Guildford, Staff Commandant Red Cross Anne, Royal Surrey County Hospital, Guildford.' She was honoured with an OBE.

LOCAL HISTORIES

In the years after the Armistice a number of councils commissioned histories of their areas during the war. They were largely uncritical accounts, but they do give a flavour of how their communities reacted to the unprecedented challenges. But they contain lots of names, particularly of councillors and those who ran the war charities and administrative bodies from pension to agricultural committees. There may also be a roll of honour for local men.

The local library should have a copies for their area and a number have been republished by Naval & Military Press.

Schools

Schools and schoolchildren were increasingly pressed into the war effort, raising money for the war charities, knitting socks or gathering items from the hedgerows and fields like sphagnum moss for use in hospitals. The most successful campaign was undoubtedly the Cornwell Memorial Fund, in memory of the 'Boy VC' Jack Cornwell, in which millions of children gave a penny each to endow beds for disabled servicemen at the Star & Garter Home in Richmond.

School activities should be recorded in logbooks kept by the head teacher. Where they survive, they are at local record offices, although a few schools may still have copies. The logs will also note the arrival and departure of individual children, including refugee children, and preparations for air raids.

Air Raids

The most immediate impact on the civilian population was the air raids. German attacks on English towns began at the end of 1914 with bombardments of Scarborough and Hartlepool by ships of the German High Fleet. The first air raid on British soil took place on 19 January 1915 over Great Yarmouth by Zeppelin L3, which dropped twelve bombs on the town. The damage the airship caused was minimal, but two local residents were killed: Samuel Smith, a cobbler aged 53, and Martha Taylor, aged 72. Later that same day Zeppelin L4 attacked King's Lynn and other towns along the coast of north Norfolk.

If your town was under attack there are likely to be records at the local record office and probably a book or two written about them. Records of the RNAS, which was tasked with defending Britain's air space, are discussed in Chapter Six.

Military Service Tribunals

With the introduction of conscription in March 1916 an appeals system was established, which allowed men, and their employers, to appeal against

A Bruce Bairnsfather cartoon reflecting the frustration many soldiers felt at the number of men supposedly excused service by the tribunals. In fact, few men avoided military service altogether unless they were engaged in work of national importance. (Author's collection)

If Only They'd Make "Old Bill" President of Those Tribunals

" Well, what's your job, me lad ?"
" Making spots for rocking-horses, sir "
"Three months"
" Exemption, sir ?"
" Nao, exemption be ——d ! Three months' hard !".

conscription. The vast majority of cases concerned employment (such as the last young man on a farm) or domestic arrangements (looking after elderly relations). Only a few related to conscientious objections against the war.

Most records were destroyed in the 1920s, with only those ones for Middlesex being preserved at TNA (series MH 47) and Midlothian at the National Records of Scotland in Edinburgh (www.nas.gov.uk). In addition, records from a few tribunals also survive at local record offices, notably Wiltshire and Cumberland. TNA's records are being indexed and digitised and should be available online in late 2014.

There is also full coverage of tribunals in local newspapers, often including verbatim accounts of meetings together with the decisions made by the tribunal. On 31 March the *Tamworth Herald*, for example, reported that two clerks, Ernest Lees and George Keys, clerks at a local colliery, claimed exemption from service because their firm had been unable to obtain an efficient lady clerk to replace them. Their appeal was rejected and both were given one month's grace before they had to join the colours.

There is an excellent TNA In-Depth Research Guide *Conscientious objectors in the First World War: further research*, which explains the system in some detail and suggests sources at Kew.

Conscientious Objectors

During the war there were 16,100 registered conscientious objectors and many more men who had serious doubts about war in general and the First World War in particular. Their position was ridiculed by the mainstream press and society in general. Some were given total exemption but the majority were placed in non-combatant corps, put to work in labour camps or on other work. Those who failed with their appeal to a tribunal were sent to fight in France. Where they continued with their objection, they were imprisoned, court-martialled or worse: 1,298 conscientious objectors were imprisoned and 41 were executed. Yet their spirit was rarely broken. One Conshie Fenner Brockway later wrote: 'I had eight months solitary confinement at Lincoln Prison. Three months bread and water treatment until the doctor wouldn't allow more. And yet one had a sense of freedom which I can't describe. . . . one had an extraordinary sense of personal liberty, personal freedom.'

Records of the courts martial of these men are at TNA in WO 90 and WO 213. However, 1,350 'absolutists' refused this compromise and were imprisoned often in appalling conditions – seventy-three of whom died while in gaol.

There is no comprehensive list of conscientious objectors. There is material about them and their resistance to war at the IWM and much at the Friends' Library (www.quaker.org.uk/library). The Friends' Library leaflet *Conscientious Objectors and the Peace Movement in Britain 1914–1945* is a useful checklist to what is available. The Peace Pledge Union (www.ppu.org.uk) also has some records and runs an educational resource. The CO Project has a checklist of primary and secondary material and details are at www.coproject.org.uk.

Internees

British in Germany

At the outbreak of war British and Commonwealth civilians resident in Germany were interned in camps, the largest of which was Ruhleben, a former racetrack on the edge of Berlin, which housed 4,500 men and women. Conditions in general were reasonable, considering the problems faced by civilians in Germany as a whole. The biggest problem was boredom, which was overcome to an extent by a network of clubs and adult education classes.

It is now difficult to find out very much about these people, although short biographies of some 1,700 internees are provided by Chris Paton at http://ruhleben.tripod.com. Some real characters were to be found in the camp. My favourite is Peter Carl Mackay, a West Indian from the Danish West Indies, who before the 1914 had been a horse trainer and circus performer. History knows him as Prince Monolulu, a colourful racing tipster and minor celebrity before and after the Second World War. A few lists and related letters can be found in the correspondence of the Foreign Office Prisoner of War Department (FO 383). Indexes to these records, including many names, can be found in TNA's Catalogue.

The deaths of internees are recorded by the CWGC.

The ICRC in Geneva was responsible for passing details of civilians (both British and German) between the various combatant nations and ensuring that conditions in the camps were adequate. Voluminous records were maintained which are closed for 100 years, however, their archivists will search the records for you. You need to contact the ICRC Archives, 19 avenue de la Paix, CH-1202 Genève, Switzerland. More information can be found at www.icrc.org. It is expected that many of these records will be online during 2014.

Germans in Britain

Some 60,000 German and Austrian citizens in Britain were interned or repatriated. The largest internment camp was at Knockaloe near Peel on the Isle of Man, which housed 24,500 people. Lists of internees are in series HO 144 and WO 900 at TNA, with related correspondence in HO 45. Personal files for these people have long been destroyed: other records are held by the Red Cross in Geneva (see above). The Manx National Heritage Library has some ephemera (listed at www.gov.im/mnh/heritage/ library/bibliographies/internment.xml), but no other records are known to survive, although there is an interesting webpage at www.isle-of-man.com/manxnotebook/fulltext/sh1920/ch06.htm with links to other sites.

War Refugees

By June 1915, it is estimated 265,000 Belgian refugees had arrived in Britain, of whom 40,000 were wounded soldiers and 15,000 were Russian Jews who had worked in the diamond industry in Antwerp. Some later returned home. A census was taken of the 211,000 refugees in Britain in June 1915, in order to determine who was suitable for military service or work in the war economy. There were 65,000 men over 16, 80,000 women over 16 and 66,000 children. Many found work in the local munitions factories (a special village, called Elisabethville, was built for the Belgian at Birtley in Country Durham) or subsisted on hand-outs from increasingly resentful charities. Almost everybody returned home within weeks of the Armistice in 1918.

They were looked after largely by local voluntary organisations under the auspices of the quasi-official War Refugees Committee. Cards about individual refugees, together with correspondence about their care, are held at TNA in series MH 8. There may well also be some material at local record offices in the papers of local war refugee committees or in school logs. There is an entry in the logbook of the Richard's Endowed School in Silverton, Devon, dated 3 March 1916: 'Admitted Victor Decorte, a Belgian boy. Though being only in England 15 months he has got on wonderfully well in English. The family have just come from Blackawton'. Another entry for 24 July 1916: 'Victor Decorte has been taken off the Register. The family (Belgian refugees) have removed to London.' (www .exetermemories.co.uk/forum/viewtopic.php?f=9&t=357).

The State Archives in Brussels also have some material (http:// arch.arch.be).

Chapter 8

THE DOMINIONS

It was not Britain alone. The British Empire played a huge part in the Allied war victory. And Gallipoli, for Australia and New Zealand, and Vimy Ridge, for Canada, were hugely important events in the building of unique identities in these nations.

The relationship was not necessarily an easy one.

When Britain declared war on 4 August 1914 she did so on behalf of the Empire as well as the United Kingdom itself. The declaration was generally warmly received. The Australian politician Andrew Fisher promised that 'Australians will stand beside [the mother country] to help and defend her to our last man and our last shilling'. Indeed, the first shots of the war fired by a British unit were across the bows of an escaping German steamer during the afternoon of 5 August from a battery at the entrance of Port Philip Bay near Melbourne.

In the early years of the war, as had been the case before 1914, foreign and defence policy was decided in Whitehall usually with only cursory consultation of the Dominions. During the war this high-handed policy intensely frustrated politicians like Canadian Prime Minister Robert Borden, who grumbled in early 1916 that, 'It can hardly be expected that we shall put 400,000 or 500,000 men in the field and willingly accept the position of having no more voice and receiving no more consideration than if we were toy automata.'

Behind the scenes there was increasing disquiet about the quality of the British High Command. In turn, the British had reservations about the relaxed attitude to discipline and relations between officers and men which were common in the forces from the Dominions. However, by 1918 Sir Arthur Currie from Canada and Sir John Monash from Australia were commanding exclusively Canadian and ANZAC corps on the Western Front respectively, reflecting both the contribution made by their nations as well as personal military qualities. Monash, who had been an estate agent in Melbourne before the war, was particularly highly regarded.

There was also the semi-autonomous Indian Empire (now India, Pakistan and Bangladesh), which was run by the British under a Viceroy. The Raj was made up of British-controlled India and a number of nominally independent native states, although here the dominant figure was always the British resident. The British Army maintained a number of garrisons in the sub-continent. In addition, there was the separate Indian Army, under the control of the Viceroy, but largely run by British officers. In the early months of the war Indian troops fought supremely well on the Western Front, winning four Victoria Crosses, but were slowly replaced by British and white Dominion troops and were relegated to fighting in Palestine and Mesopotamia (Iraq).

Lastly, there were dozens of smaller colonies, some of which had been British since the seventeenth century, while others in Africa and the Pacific had been annexed fairly recently. Most were poor and generally contributed little to the war effort. Here local enthusiasm was often dampened by the refusal of the British authorities to allow Colonial troops near the front line, in Europe at least, although there were several battalions of West Indian and Chinese labourers, or to allow 'persons of colour', as they were termed, to become officers. You will see on application forms for commissions that applicants had to state that they were of pure European stock.

A large proportion of Dominion forces were made up of British-born men who had emigrated overseas before the war, but still felt a loyalty to the mother country. Two-thirds of the men in the Canadian forces at Vimy Ridge are thought to have been born in the British Isles. In addition, a fair number of British men endeavoured to join these units, largely because pay and conditions were better than in the British Army as a whole. Conversely, Dominion-born men, who may have been working or studying in Britain, enlisted in British units.

With the exception of the Indian Army, contingents from the Dominions and Colonies were regarded as being part of the British Army. The records thus created are very similar to those you may be familiar with when researching British servicemen. Indeed, there are some shared records:

- The CWGC records the last resting place of all Dominion and Colonial troops.

- Gallantry awards and the commissions and promotion of officers in Dominion and Colonial forces appear in the *London Gazette*. Apart from Canada, few of the official gazettes from the Dominions, let alone the Colonies, are yet online, so this is a useful alternative. TNA also has a complete set of these official gazettes.

- Some war diaries for Dominion, Indian and Colonial units are at TNA in series WO 95.

One unique series of records, however, are the embarkation rolls which record the departure and return of service personnel from the shores of

Australia, New Zealand and Canada. The records will tell you in which unit an individual was serving, the ship they were on and where they departed or arrived, and possibly other information as well.

There were once equivalents for British forces, but they have largely been destroyed. Occasionally, regimental archives may have sets for their battalions. TNA has a selection of embarkation returns in series WO 25, which lists where units were despatched and when and where they went. Officers are listed but other ranks are not. The records are not indexed, but they are arranged roughly by date of departure.

Because of the iconic status of the First World War in the national myths of Australia, New Zealand and Canada considerable resources have been devoted to putting material online. In addition, these databases are normally free to access.

Australia

The National Archives of Australia holds service documents for, among other formations, the 1st Australian Imperial Force (AIF), Australian Flying Corps, Australian Army Nursing Service, and Depot or home records for personnel who served within Australia. The records are online, free of charge, at www.naa.gov.au/collection/explore/defence/service-records/army-wwi.aspx and you can download high-quality images for a small fee. It is not terribly easy to use. Also available are Navy service records, which typically consist of one or two cardboard index cards with indistinct pencil notations.

Indeed, it might be worth starting with the AIF Project, which is easier to use and obtain basic information from. The Project was set up by the Australian Defence Force Academy and lists the details of those who served overseas with the AIF (www.aif.adfa.edu.au).

The Australian equivalent of the IWM is the Australian War Memorial (AWM, www.awm.gov.au), which has a superb collection of material relating to Australian forces since 1901. Many records have been indexed or digitised and placed online free of charge. These include:

- A roll of honour with some personnel details, based on forms supplied by next of kin to the AWM after the First World War.

- First World War Embarkation Roll which contains details of approximately 330,000 AIF personnel as they left Australia for overseas service.

- First World War Nominal Roll which has details of 324,000 AIF personnel, recorded to assist with their repatriation to Australia from overseas service.

The attestation papers for Private Thomas Linton, Australian Imperial Force. Both he and his brother William were killed in separate incidents on the same day, 31 March 1917. (National Archives of Australia)

- Honours and awards with details of approximately 59,000 recommendations for Honours and awards made to members of the AIF.

- Australian Red Cross Wounded and Missing Enquiry Bureau files for 32,000 Australian servicemen reported as wounded or missing.

If you are ever in Canberra, the AWM is definitely well worth visiting.

Canada

Library and Archives Canada holds many records for men and women who served in the Canadian forces during the First World War. A proportion of these are available online through the Collections Canada portal (www.collectionscanada.ca). Unfortunately, the databases are not always easy to use and the information available partial. Before you start it might be worth looking at their First World War Search Topic, which explains what is available, at www.collectionscanada.gc.ca/genealogy/022-909.006-e.html.

In particular, the personnel records for the 600,000 Canadians who enlisted in the Canadian Expeditionary Force (CEF) are available online. Unfortunately, the records have been heavily weeded, and only key documents survive. You can obtain the full service record for a fee, although attestation papers are available, free of charge, at www.collectionscanada.gc.ca/genealogy/022-909.006-e.html. Also available are war diaries for Canadian units.

The Canadian Virtual War Memorial, www.vac-acc.gc.ca/remembers/sub.cfm?source=collections/virtualmem, contains details of Canadians who died in the war and their last resting place. The information is similar to that available from the CWGC. In addition, the website also has pages about Canada during the First World War. Possibly of more use are the Circumstances of Death files for individuals, which are available at www.ancestry.ca (British subscribers will need to pay extra to use databases here), although unindexed records are available on the Collections Canada website.

Service records for members of the Royal Canadian Navy and Volunteer Reserve are with Library and Archives Canada. Also worth looking at are the Service Ledgers. Details of honours and awards to Canadian naval personnel can be found at www.rcnvr.com.

Further Reading

Glenn Wright, *Canadians at War 1914–1918: A Research Guide to War Service Records*, Global Genealogy Press, 2010.

India

Some 1.4 million Indians served during the war in the Indian Army, which was under the command of British officers. Where the service records of the Indian servicemen are is not known. However, the BL (www.bl.uk) inherited the official records of the British Raj in India, including records of the Indian Army. As a result, it has material relating to the service of officers. Unfortunately, there are many different, and at times

An Indian Mountain Artillery Battery in action. (W D Downes, With the Nigerians in East Africa, *Methuen, 1919)*

duplicating, sources, which can present problems in researching Indian Army officers.

Perhaps the best place to start is with an online database (http://indiafamily.bl.uk/UI/) to British civil and military employees living in India, but this is by no means complete

Another easy to use source is the India Army List, which is very similar to the British Army Lists. The BL has a set of these volumes on open shelves in the African and Asian Studies Reading Room at their St Pancras site. You must obtain a reader's ticket before using any material at the BL. However, commercial data providers have digitised odd volumes.

Service records for officers and warrant officers in the Indian Army only begin in 1900 and continue to 1950. They are to be found in series IOL L/MIL/14 at the BL. There is an index to names available online through the A2A database (www.nationalarchives.gov.uk/a2a). You will, however, need to filter the search by repository, i.e., BL and perhaps by date.

Application forms for Wellington and Quetta cadets of the Indian Army (1915–18) are in pieces L/MIL/9/320-32, and include details of the cadet, his family background and age. An index can be found within each volume.

TNA has some records including war diaries from a number of Indian units in WO 95. They are mainly for units which served in Mesopotamia and Palestine.

TNA's Online Records Service service includes medal index cards for over 20,000 soldiers, mainly officers who served in the Indian Army. They contain much the same information as the cards for members of the British Army, although the medal rolls to which they refer no longer survive. These cards are not available on Ancestry.

The NAM (www.nam.ac.uk) also has a large collection of material for the Indian Army. The highlight is probably Major Hobson's 'Card Index to Indian Officers and Civilians', which includes details of men in the Indian Army at the time of the First World War.

Further Reading

The records are difficult to use and before you start it is a good idea to consult the following:

Emma Jolly, *Tracing Your British Indian Ancestors*, Pen & Sword, 2010.

Ian Baxter, *Baxter's Guide: Biographical Sources in the India Office Records*, 3rd edn, FIBIS, 2004.

Indian Army officer casualties are described in S B and D B Jarvis, *The Cross of Sacrifice: Officers Who Died in the Service of the British, Indian and East African Regiments and Corps, 1914–1919*, Naval & Military Press, 1993.

The Families in British India Society (FIBIS) has many resources available online as well as a very useful wiki at www.fibis.org.

Newfoundland

Until 1949 Newfoundland was separate from Canada and this is reflected in the records. However, there were close links between the two countries, so researchers may need to use Canadian sources as well.

Surviving service records of the Newfoundland Regiment are with the Provincial Archives of Newfoundland and Labrador in St John's, and fully available online free of charge at www.therooms.ca/regiment/part3_database.asp.

A number of Newfoundlanders enlisted in the RNR and records of the Reserve are described in Chapter 5. A useful website describing Newfoundland's experience of the war is at www.heritage.nf.ca/greatwar/articles/regiment.html.

New Zealand

Personnel records of nearly 120,000 men who served in the New Zealand Expeditionary Force and were discharged before the end of 1920 are held

The first page of the service record for Corporal Thomas Buxton, NZEF. (Archives New Zealand)

by Archives New Zealand. They are similar to those of other Dominions. You can download service records, free of charge, at http://archway.archives.govt.nz, alt. In addition, the Archives New Zealand has nominal casualty rolls, rolls of honour, unit (war) diaries and records relating to honours and awards. They are briefly described in a research guide at http://archives.govt.nz/research/guides/war#first.

Auckland War Memorial Museum's Cenotaph Database is in effect a roll of honour for New Zealand service personnel. It is online at http://muse.aucklandmuseum.com/databases/cenotaph and can be searched by name, place or troopship. Unusually, it contains more information than is to be found with the CWGC and, usefully, there are links to the individual's service record at Archives New Zealand. Casualty cards for 700 Kiwis who were killed during the Battle of Passchendaele between July and November 1917 are online at www.archives.govt.nz/exhibitions/passchendaele/?start=E&y=285. A database of war memorials in New Zealand with photographs, although no lists of names, is at www.nzhistory.net.nz/culture/the-memorials-register.

http://freepages.genealogy.rootsweb.com/~sooty is a general New Zealand genealogy website with pages from the New Zealand Expeditionary Force's roll of honour and much else about the Kiwi war effort during the First World War.

South Africa

Service records are held by the South African National Defence Force, which can be contacted at Documentation Service, Private Bag X289, Pretoria 0001, South Africa. There seems to be almost nothing online about men who served in the South African forces during the First World War.

Colonies

The majority of the Colonies were too small to do more than raise a local militia and send small financial contributions to London. Several Colonial regiments saw action, the Nigerian Regiment as part of the West African Field Force and the King's African Rifles in German East Africa (now Tanzania) and the West India Regiment in Cameroon. The West India Regiment also later served on the Western Front engaged on labour duties. No service records appear to survive for these regiments, but basic details can be picked up from the medal index cards.

Many of the men impressed their officers with their bravery. Of Company Sergeant Major Belo Akure, 4th Nigerian Regiment serving in East Africa, his commanding officer, Captain William Downes, later wrote:

This sergeant-major is a most remarkable native . . . He was awarded

Company Sergeant Major Belo Akure DCM*, MM of the Nigerian Regiment, which fought in East Africa. (W D Downes, With the Nigerians in East Africa, *Methuen, 1919)*

The medal index card for Belo Akure. (Ancestry)

his bar [to his DCM] for covering the retreat of a party of Nigerians by checking the enemy's advance by himself. He was ordered to conduct the retirement of an advance post that was being heavily attacked. The post was separated from the main position by an unfordable river 35 yards in width. He got his men into the only available canoe, and finding that it would founder if he got in himself, he lay on the bank and covered their retirement, being all the time subjected to heavy fire himself, one bullet actually cutting his sleeve. When his men landed he ordered them into the trenches on the other side of the stream, and then swam the river himself under heavy fire to join them. I . . . can honestly state that I have never seen a braver man. It makes one feel quite ashamed of oneself when that nasty feeling of fear catches one deep down inside and has to be expelled, for one realizes that this native does not know what the feeling of fear is. (W D Downes, *With the Nigerians in East Africa*, Methuen, 1919, pp. 104–5)

Akure was heavily decorated with a Distinguished Conduct Medal and bar as well as a Military Medal. Unfortunately, I have been unable to find any mention of the DCM or the bar in the *London Gazette* or Findmypast's index to DCM citations.

Officers of the King's African Rifles and other units raised in East Africa are described in S B and D B Jarvis, *The Cross of Sacrifice: Officers Who Died in the Service of the British, Indian and East African Regiments and Corps, 1914–1919*, Naval & Military Press, 1993. More about the role of West Indian and African troops can be found at ww.mgtrust.org/afr1.htm. The story of the Fijian war effort is told at www.freewebs.com/fiji, with particular reference to the European population, who sent a company of men to join the British Army.

Appendix 1

USEFUL ADDRESSES

British Library, 96 Euston Road, London NW1 2DB; www.bl.uk

Fleet Air Arm Museum, RNAS Yeovilton, Ilchester BA22 8HT; www.fleetairarm.com

Imperial War Museum, Lambeth Road, London SE1 6HZ; www.iwm.org.uk.

The National Archives, Ruskin Avenue, Kew, Richmond TW9 4DU; www.nationalarchives.gov.uk

National Army Museum, Royal Hospital Road, London SW3 4HT; www.national-army-museum.org.uk

National Maritime Museum, Romney Road, Greenwich, London SE10 9NF; www.nmm.ac.uk

RAF Museum, Graeme Park Way, London NW9 5LL; www.rafmuseum.org.uk

Royal Naval Museum, H M Naval Base, Portsmouth PO1 3NH; www.royalnavalmuseum.org/research.htm

Service Personnel and Veterans Agency, Norcross, Thornton Cleveleys FY5 3WP; www.veterans-uk.info

Appendix 2

KEY WEBSITES

These are the most important websites you will use in your research. They are all described fully in the book.

Ancestry – www.ancestry.co.uk

Findmypast – www.findmypast.co.uk

The National Archives – www.nationalarchives.gov.uk

London Gazette – www.london-gazette.co.uk

Commonwealth War Graves Commission – www.cwgc.org

British Newspaper Archive – www.britishnewspaperarchive.co.uk

Regimental museums and archives – www.army-museums.org.uk

Long, Long Trail – www.1914-1918.net

Naval-History.Net – www.naval-history.net

Appendix 3

HOW THE ARMY WAS ORGANISED

Army Structure

Army

Largest sub-division of the British Army (250,000–350,000 men) commanded by a general.

Corps

Each army was split into 3–6 corps, each corps normally had 4 divisions with each commanded by a lieutenant general.

There were also (unrelated) specialist corps, most notably the RA and Royal Engineers, but also medical, veterinary and the Army Service Corps. Typically, they were divided into companies or batteries commanded by a captain or major.

Division

Each division had roughly 18,000 men and was commanded by a major general.

Brigade

Sub-division of a division (typically there were 3 or 4 brigades in each division). It was commanded by a brigadier general.

There were also artillery brigades which were split into four batteries.

Regiment

Before 1916 regiments were largely recruited from a specific locality and so built up close links with a particular district. Men in the Connaught

Rangers, for example, largely came from the West of Ireland, and the Royal Fusiliers from London.

In peacetime there were normally 2 battalions, 1 stationed at home with the other overseas, normally in India, with 1 or 2 additional territorial or volunteer battalions made up of part-time soldiers. Between 1914 and 1918 there was a huge increase in battalions which is reflected in their nomenclature and numbering. Initially, men who joined in the early months of the war were put into service battalions, generally numbered between 8 and 13.

Often battalions were split into 2 or more, something that is reflected in their numbering. Thus the 2/8 Sherwood Foresters is the second battalion created from the 8th Battalion (and is referred to as being the 'second eighth'). The 8th Battalion was a service battalion, formed in Newark on 11 September 1914.

During the war the regiment had a much less fixed role, perhaps providing basic training at the regimental depot, a focus for local charitable effort sending parcels to men at the front or in prisoner of war camps.

Battalion Organisation

The battalion was the basic infantry unit. Initially, almost all recruits joined one of these battalions, but by the end of war as the result of increasing mechanisation most men were members of one of the specialist branches, such as the Artillery or Machine Gun Corps.

At full establishment (which was rare), the battalion consisted of 1,007 men, of whom 30 were officers. It comprised a battalion HQ and 4 companies.

It was usually commanded by a lieutenant colonel with a major as second-in-command. Battalion HQ also had 3 other officers: an adjutant (in charge of battalion administration), the quartermaster (responsible for stores and transport) and a medical officer attached from the RAMC.

Battalion HQ also included a regimental sergeant major, who was the most senior NCO, together with specialist tradesmen: quartermaster, drummer, cook, pioneer, shoemaker, transport, signaller, armourer (often attached from the Army Ordnance Corps) and orderly room clerk.

A corporal and 15 privates were employed in a special Signalling Section (often the brightest men in the battalion or men thought to have the potential to become officers); 10 privates were employed as pioneers (on construction, repair and general engineering duties); 11 privates acted as drivers for the transport; 16 (later 32) men acted as stretcher-bearers (who were often musicians from the battalion band); and finally 6 privates acted as officers' batmen (personal servants) and 2 were orderlies for the medical officer.

Companies comprised 227 officers and men at full establishment. Each company was referred by a letter, A–D. They were commanded by a major or captain, with a captain as second-in-command. Company HQ included a company sergeant major, a company quartermaster sergeant, 2 batmen and 3 drivers. The company was divided into 4 platoons, each of which was commanded by a subaltern (a lieutenant or second lieutenant).

Each platoon was subdivided into 4 sections, each of 12 men under an NCO. For most men the section was the centre of their world, they fought together and lived and grumbled together.

In addition, in 1914 each battalion had a machine-gun section consisting of a lieutenant, a sergeant, a corporal, 2 drivers, a batman and 12 privates trained in the maintenance, transport, loading and firing of the Vickers heavy machine gun. These men made up 2 6-man gun teams.

Each battalion had a detachment at its base depot, which did not take the field when the battalion was on active service. In theory, the base detachment consisted of a subaltern, 2 sergeants and just under 100 privates to form a first reinforcement (to make good battalion casualties or other losses); four storemen, the band sergeant and the sergeant master tailor. When the battalion went on active service, it left behind the bandmaster and the sergeant instructor of musketry for service with the reserve battalion.

The reality in the trenches was often very different. In particular, it was rare for a battalion to be at full strength.

By February 1915 the allocation of machine guns to each battalion had been doubled to 4. A year later the gunners were formally transferred to the new Machine Gun Corps, as happened to Lance Corporal Byers, who moved from the 6th Highland Light Infantry in Egypt to a MGC battalion. In return, battalions received 4 Lewis light machine guns. By the Battle of the Somme this had been increased to 16 guns per battalion, and early in 1918 this again increased to 36 guns.

Battle experience also led to battalions leaving behind a cadre of men (a mix of instructors, trained signallers and other specialists) to form a nucleus for rebuilding, in the event of heavy casualties.

Based on David Borrill, *Great War Family Ancestry Research Booklet*, self-published, 2001 and Chris Baker's Long, Long Trail website (www.1914-1918.net/whatbatt.htm).

Comparative Rank Structure between the Various Services

Officers

Army	Navy	RNAS	RAF
	Midshipman		
Second Lieutenant	Sub Lieutenant	Flight Sub Lieutenant	Pilot Officer
Lieutenant	Lieutenant	Flight Lieutenant	Flying Officer
Captain	Lieutenant	Flight Commander	Flight Lieutenant
Major	Lieutenant Commander	Squadron Commander	Squadron Leader
Lieutenant Colonel	Commander	Wing Commander	Wing Commander
Colonel	Captain		Group Captain
Brigadier General	Commodore		Air Commodore
Major General	Rear Admiral		Air Vice Marshal
Lieutenant General	Vice Admiral		Air Marshal
General	Admiral		Air Chief Marshal
Field Marshal	Admiral of the Fleet		Marshal of the RAF

Non-commissioned Officers and Other Ranks

Army	Navy	RAF
Sergeant Major	Warrant Officer	Flight Sergeant
Sergeant	Chief Petty Officer	Sergeant
Corporal	Petty Officer	Corporal
Lance Corporal	Leading Rating	Leading Aircraftsman
Private/Gunner/ Bombadier/Sapper	Rating	Aircraftsman

RAF ranks were not adopted until 1919. During 1918 the new service used Army ranks. The exact terminology for Army other ranks varied slightly between regiments and corps.

156

Appendix 4

BATTLEFIELD TOURISM

There has been a huge increase in tourism to the Western Front over the past two decades or so. With the Channel Tunnel and an impressive motorway network it is now an easy day trip from London. The roads are generally good and the major attractions easy to find, with a range of hotels, bars and restaurants to suit most pockets. There are a number of tour companies that organise trips, but it is perfectly possible to construct your own itinerary, although if you are thinking of going further afield than 'France and Flanders' then it might be wise to use a tour company. The websites described below offer some guidance as well as providing other information about the Western Front then and now.

Hellfire Corner at www.fylde.demon.co.uk/welcome.htm has an off-putting home page, but many articles about visiting the Western Front, war memorials, tracing individual soldiers as well as links to the webmaster's military book shop at www.ww1battlefields.co.uk, which has pages about travel to the Western Front today, but is perhaps best for the pages of reviews of books about the war.

www.battlefield-tours.com is mainly a site for a battlefield tours company, but there are some additional interesting pages relating to the Somme and Ypres.

If your interest is the Somme rather than Flanders, the www.somme-battlefields.co.uk/en is a good place to start with plenty of advice for potential visitors. While there, one place to call in at is Avril Williams' B&B and tearoom at Auchonvilliers on the Somme, details at www.avril-williams.com. While there make sure you visit the cellar with its original wartime graffiti.

Phil Curme visits battlefields (not just First World War ones) on holiday. His website www.curme.co.uk/index.htm contains his holiday snaps and musings, and is better than it sounds!

Although hard to read, http://user.glo.be/~snelders/contents.html is an excellent practical site about Gallipoli and how to get there and what to see when you do. There are lots of pages about the campaign such as the weather and notes of a visit to the peninsula in 1934.

There are dozens of companies, large and small, that offer tours to the Western Front and other sites. It is a good idea to choose organisations that use members of the Guild of Battlefield Guides because you will be guaranteed a high level of knowledge and the ability to express it; a rather out of date list of members can be found on the Guild's website www.gbg-international.com.

The largest, and certainly the oldest, in the field is Holts, www.holts.co.uk. Another sizeable company is Leger, www.leger.co.uk/Experiences/Battlefields. Smaller companies, however, can offer a more personalised service, but of course don't go to as many places. The Battlefield Experience, for example, specialises in the Somme, thebattleofthesomme.co.uk. Flanders Battlefield Tours (which I can thoroughly recommend) looks after Ypres, ypres-fbt.com. Another company I have worked with, and can recommend, is Matt Limb Battlefield Tours (www.mlbft.co.uk). If you are a member of the WFA, many companies advertise in *Stand To!* and the Association and its branches also run the occasional tour.

INDEX